# The Ninefold Path

. . . . . . .

*A Memoir*

ANTHONY M. ALIOTO

**TURNING
STONE
PRESS**

First published in 2012 by
Turning Stone Press, an imprint of
Red Wheel/Weiser, LLC
With offices at:
665 Third Street, Suite 400
San Francisco, CA 94107
*www.redwheelweiser.com*

ISBN (paperback): 978-1-61852-037-1
ISBN (hardcover): 978-1-61852-036-4

Cover design by Jim Warner
Cover art by Luciano Alioto

Printed in the United States of America
IBT
10 9 8 7 6 5 4 3 2 1

# Contents

# Note to the Reader

This is the sort of memoir one would rather forget. Yet at this precise moment, there are thousands, perhaps tens of thousands, who are about to undertake the *journey* described here. There are families, friends, lovers, acquaintances, and others who will take the journey with them. Whatever its specific nature, chronic illness is a long, creeping shadow that gradually envelops one's life as well as the lives of innocent onlookers. It is as if the moment of death extends over an agonizing length of time.

This memoir is for you, sufferers and onlookers.

Here is the story of one person's journey from health to illness, and back to a kind of health. Specifically, it is a memoir about the "slow death" of kidney failure due to hypertension. It is a first-hand account of modern medicine, dialysis, and finally renal transplant. It is the story of how one becomes a marginal person, neither healthy nor totally incapacitated. It is a lesson in denial, the futility of "kicking against the goad."

The reader can expect to encounter a very personal account of chronic illness, sometimes painful, sometimes hilarious, and then at times simply absurd—but, hopefully, also moving. One need not search for profound insights, recipes, therapy, or sage advice. It is my hope that you will come away with a feeling, a sense of being there, maybe a kind of liberation from the "merely personal," as Einstein phrased it, a new appreciation for what others endure daily. To the latter: Even in the midst of suffering, physical pain and mental anguish, a person may yet gain the freedom to live a life of celebration, joy, compassion, and serenity. Zen Master Kyong Ho once said: "Don't hope for life without problems. An easy life results in a judgmental and lazy mind."

Still, these truly are memories I would prefer to forget. But that is impossible. I have been forced to reach a modus vivendi with myself since my health was restored by the death of a child. My new kidney, my new life, came at the impossible, frightful cost of a child's death. Therefore, I *must* share the story. But, a point I cannot emphasize enough, *this is a single individual's account*. Others may well perceive the same things in total opposition to my perspective. Let these "others" consider the Buddhist philosopher Nagarjuna: Light is interdependent with darkness, to have light is to have darkness, darkness light.

Tsar Alexander III of Russia had the physique of a Russian bear with the strength to match. Yet, in the spring of 1894, this powerful autocrat only in his mid-forties began to suffer some indefinable disease. He grew steadily weaker as he battled insomnia, loss of appetite and a steady drain of his vitality. On October 20, at 2:15 p.m., he died, leaving the troubled Russian Empire in the incapable hands of his son, Nicholas II, who possessed mere "infantile judgment." War and revolution soon followed.

Tsar Alexander III died of kidney failure. Dialysis had yet to be invented. Transplant belonged in the realm of science fiction, a subject for the macabre on the order of Frankenstein.

I was an athlete of sorts, a distance runner. Like the tsar, no one, especially me, would have suspected the small deaths occurring in my kidneys. Like the tsar, the illness became apparent only after it was too late to halt its destruction. Unlike the tsar, modern medicine rescued me from certain death.

You are invited to endure a sometimes harrowing, but ultimately life-giving encounter with modern medicine. In these pages, like the "seer behind seeing" of the ancient Hindu *Upanishads*, you will experience dialysis, surgeries, enough needles to fill a haystack, near death episodes at the mindless whim of the dialysis machine (and my own stupidity), and the sadness yet exhilaration of transplant. You learn "the drill," as they say.

Most people suffering from some illness, be it as benign as a blister or as life-threatening as cancer, usually ask the physician or nurse: "What can I expect?" The medical professionals generally provide good, competent answers detailing the technical aspects of the treatment as well as the statistical results. But unless they have experienced the procedures for themselves, there is usually something, maybe just a tiny burr, that is missing. And these small imperfections can make a tremendous difference. Read every information pamphlet the hospital provides and yet you still may find yourself wondering: "What can I expect?"

This account locates my perception of the rough edges and *does not smooth them over*. Use this book as a guide, a map by which to navigate the landscape of modern medicine. But do not confuse the map with the ground. In the end, every experience is unique, and *all comparisons are false*.

The equation is reversible. All good health professionals are constantly trying to understand and deal with what the patient is feeling, the patient's psychology, no matter how irrational it may appear. I have been invited by hospitals and other professional organizations to give talks about my experience. Invariably, the question arises: "What can we do to improve patient care?" Hopefully, this memoir will make some worthwhile suggestions.

The same holds for loved ones and friends. Your suffering is no less real; entire families suffer the chronic illness. Your pain is no less intense, sometimes greater.

∼

When is the right time to die? The question may not be as strange as it seems. Today we hear about "end of life," "right to life," or "quality of life." A college professor, I was able to "work" while on dialysis. What this demonstrates about the work involved in college teaching I leave to the reader's judgment. I could use "making a contribution to society" as a reason (excuse?) to go on with a frightfully costly treatment. To be honest, one would have to poll students on the effectiveness of this excuse.

The question haunts me even today. Treatment gobbled up huge amounts of resources that might have been used more wisely. The fact is, however, that most people facing a life-threatening illness are consumed by the frantic desire to do anything, submit to anything, spend anything, inconvenience anybody to keep breathing. I was no different. Keep me going no matter what the expense! I still feel there is something slightly sinister about this attitude.

Ultimately we are brought to ethical and religious (spiritual) questions. This memoir is the lived experience of a particular (peculiar) individual who has studied, and attempts to teach, the intellectual disciplines that deal with such questions. What of suffering? Life and death? Is there some cosmic meaning to it all? A purpose? Are such questions a waste of time (probably)?

It is one thing to offer intellectual answers or logical solutions. It is quite another to *feel* these questions deep in one's diseased organs, in the death of a child that also gives life. The goal of this account is to look deeply, past the rhetoric and endless advice, to gaze through the maudlin homilies that appeal to cheap sympathies. This is a pilgrim's report after all, a traveler's journal from that eerie country which is on everyone's itinerary. As the Greek novelist Nikos Kazantzakis wrote: "I call upon my memory to remember, I assemble my life from the air, place myself soldier-like before the general, and make my Report to Greco."

∼

A word on the history of this history. I have never been good at keeping diaries. Notes have a habit of disappearing, or I might find them years later stuck in the back of some old book. It is still difficult to pin down the exact moment—I believe it was in the summer of 1992—when high blood pressure and kidney failure were diagnosed. Most of my sources were preserved more by accident than design. These are mostly medical records, fragments of personal logs, and, significant only in hindsight, the steady decline in race times.

This is not to say that the memoir arises from the fog of a fragile memory. For years, I exchanged notes with an old friend—I'll call him Yakob—who lived in another part of the country. Sometime in the nineties, we discovered that marvelous (and devilish) medium called email. Emails seem to exist eternally somewhere in the ether. It was probably the slow piling up of electronic epistles that first gave me the idea for the memoir. Without Yakob's sympathetic participation I'm not sure this book would be possible.

~

What does it all mean? I guess, in the end, I still wonder. Many of the people who appear in these pages—they are composites so as not to cause more suffering—have become strangers. A significant stranger remains that rather crooked individual who struggles through the narrative. He lives in my memory, and my dreams. He, too, is a kind of composite. Like Zen Master Tenkei says, "He seems to suggest there *is something to tell*, and yet he does not say it: This is the gap a teacher leaves."

The book is for all those wearily treading the many paths bearing the street sign: Chronic Illness. The book is for those around the bedside, wondering what to do. The book is for all those who stood close to me and despaired. The book is for the passing crowd, mildly curious about the dark journey, indeed, hoping to avoid it.

Most of all, this book is for those who have dedicated their lives to health care. You are the noblest people on earth; you have given of yourselves, your energy, your very being, to relieve the suffering of strangers. Such is the greatest of all human endeavors, before which all other occupations pale in significance. For you, the healers, there is not enough praise in this world, or in the heavens.

# Preface

That nauseating headache is back. Neck and shoulder muscles pull tight as if fastened by bolts and screws. The headache clasps down to the forehead; the screws have become iron clamps. Nothing can be done. No drug will loosen the muscles. Roughly ten years ago, identical headaches were the first indication of chronic illness.

I'm just off dialysis. It is 11 a.m. on a Wednesday. This morning, around 6:15, I arrived at the dialysis clinic to wait with other patients in an anteroom until my assigned nurse came to escort me into the hemo-dialysis unit, a cavernous room of machines and large, sky-blue chairs.

By 6:30, if the "sticking" goes smoothly, I'm on the machine. For the next three and a half hours, the machine circulates my blood through a labyrinth of plastic tubing and filters, removing toxins from my body, partially replacing my failed kidneys. Without this treatment, three days a week, three and a half hours a session, I'd be dead in a week—at best, three. I'm on a short leash.

The doctors say the fluid shifts during treatment cause the headaches—not always, but frequently. In a few hours, the machine must filter the excess fluids healthy kidneys process every hour of every day. On dialysis one fondly recalls the feeling of a full bladder and the precious act of urination.

Hence the headaches, washed-out feeling, nausea, overall stress on the body—but ten years ago the cause was something quite different. Then I suffered headaches due to hypertension. The headaches, ten years ago or today, are indistinguishable.

∽

Every dialysis headache brings with it a nagging question: How did I get into such a mess?

The medical profession possesses excellent rational answers: My father suffered from End Stage Renal Disease, ESRD (irritable kidney patients often find the medical penchant for acronyms annoying). Yet my father labored his entire life in the Navy and heavy industry, handling toxic chemicals. To the day he died, he blamed the destruction of his kidneys upon environmental causes. Now we realize that genetic factors probably play a more significant role. Our kidney failures were caused by hypertension, ninety percent of which is inherited. Not knowing these facts, I lived under a false sense of security.

This illusion was born of other factors. I do not work in heavy industry; rather, I float through my days, a college professor, teaching at most twelve hours a week. I ran marathons and other distance races for over twenty years. Long distance runners, we are told, should not suffer hypertension. While running, the blood pressure increases; afterward it falls, usually lower than normal. Mine, apparently, remained elevated.

Sometime in my teens, perhaps it was seventeen or eighteen, I read Hermann Hesse's *Siddhartha*. Since that time I studied and practiced Buddhism, meditating regularly. These days we are told by self-satisfied, smiling popular gurus that, among other benefits, mindfulness helps lower blood pressure. Thus have I heard *on Oprah*, if I remember, a slick Buddhist teacher brag about his age, how young he looked and how mindfulness was a cure for stress. Much later did I realize—thanks to the true Buddhist "teaching" of my own illness—how unenlightened, how mesmerized by the ego-self many of these so-called modern saviors are. More on that later.

My blood pressure remained elevated.

Some fifty million Americans suffer from hypertension. Every year, high blood pressure causes more than fifteen thousand new cases of kidney failure in the United States (over a hundred thousand people are on dialysis in the United States, more than twice that number around the world). Diagnosed with hypertension, one is advised to lose weight, exercise, cut down on alcohol, salt, eat less meat and fat. Running a marathon of twenty-six miles, three hundred and eighty-five yards in two-and-a-half hours (my time) generally requires an excessively healthy lifestyle. And I was excessive!

Yet I had hypertension, and there were hardly any symptoms. Thus I foolishly—combined with excessive hubris—avoided medical checkups. Then, in the late 1980s, came the frightful headaches. Finally, in the spring of 1992, I went to a migraine specialist. By the time I found the right specialist, the chronic high blood pressure had severely damaged my kidneys' blood vessels (reducing blood flow and thus the organ's ability to filter waste products) and nephrons (the structural unit of the kidneys performing the mechanical filtration).

Tests performed in August and September of 1992 revealed that upwards of sixty percent of my kidney function had been permanently lost. I was immediately placed on blood pressure medicine.

With pressures under control, the renal physician advised optimism. "You're not your father," he said.

I heard that one.

What I chose not to hear was, "Of course destructive processes once begun in the kidneys usually continue to complete failure. No one knows why."

This prophetic renal oracle I ignored. For me, a kind of anti-Oedipal renal syndrome did quite nicely. *I was not my father! Nor, witnessing his dialysis battles, did I ever want to be!*

By May of 1993 renal prophecy could no longer be denied: A four-hour Glomerular Filtration Rate (GFR) test established beyond doubt kidney death. I was injected with a low dose of radioactive material acting as a marker in the blood and urine. Hourly urine samples revealed the amount filtered by the kidneys; blood samples drawn from a catheter in the arm measured the amount remaining in the blood. More in the blood and less in the urine means kidney failure. My ratio indicated declining function.

I came home nauseated and depressed—with a headache—only to find one of my manuscripts returned with a nasty rejection note (the novel was eventually published and has since gone out of print). My blood pressure began to inch up. I ignored it and went for a run (mindfully). I was not my father (illusion).

Roughly five-and-a-half years later, on Monday, September 14, 1998, I stumbled into the dialysis clinic for my first treatment. I had come to the end . . . End Stage Renal Disease.

∾

During my journey through chronic illness, I maintained a kind of personal log, haphazardly jotted notes, mostly those emails to Yakob (and his replies), recording as if in a laboratory experiment the bare facts of the case. Only now, after a decade has passed, am I foolhardy enough to attempt some meaningful interpretation.

Memoirs are not autobiographies. A memoir, says Gore Vidal in *Palimpsest*, is how one remembers a life. Autobiography is history, requiring research, checking the facts, establishing the dates and the causal flow of events. Sometimes I wonder if the distinction is all that sharp. History, too, may be a kind of professional memoir: how and what the historian remembers.

And how does one remember? Surely memory is hitched to present experience. Today, under the spell of dialysis, driven by headache, the constant throb of pain has churned the sluggish pool of memory. What can be learned from the memory of a chronic disease?

The philosopher Friedrich Nietzsche, a fellow headache sufferer, says that in the mountains the shortest way is from peak to peak. But for this path one must have long legs. Memory in these idle moments, befuddled by pain, is like this. A memoir is leaping from mountain peak to mountain peak, recalling significant experiences. To change the metaphor: A memoir is wave crests on the surface of the boundless ocean in endless motion—the always changing, moving peaks of life.

But maybe the true story haunts those dark, misty valleys? Perhaps I need to point my light down, into the depths?

This memoir represents pieces of memory, musing, while awaiting a kidney transplant. Here are fragments of images and thoughts, experiences, observations—the tissue of life torn apart by chronic illness.

I call it *The Ninefold Path*. Why this odd title?

~

Twenty-five hundred years ago, near the ancient Indian town of Gaya, a young prince named Siddhartha Gautama of the Sakya Clan found a tranquil spot beneath a sacred fig tree. There he seated himself and vowed, "Let my body rot, my bones be reduced to ashes, but I will not get up until I've found the way beyond decay and death."

We are told that the moon arose, the first full moon of the first month of spring. Beneath this moon, firm in his determination, the prince passed into meditation. Legend—another sort of memoir—tells us the results of this important ancient night. The Hindu god of illusion, Mara, vainly tried to distract the prince and get him to break his vow. But the dawn came, Venus appeared, a breeze came up and showered the seated one with blossoms.

Siddhartha awoke. He'd "blown out" the last shreds of ego-illusion. In Sanskrit the term "blown out" is usually translated as Nirvana. Siddhartha had become the Buddha, the Awakened One.

Mara, the legends tell, came back and saluted him: "Well, Buddha, you've seen and done what no one else has seen and done. But what now? How can you bear the company of others? Who among the ignorant people can grasp your experience? You'll be treated as a fool, laughed at."

Mara told the truth. Yet, the Buddha went out into the world, knowing that he would ultimately fail. He nonetheless gave voice to what could not be set in flimsy words. His compassion for the suffering of all sentient beings drove him on. His compassion demonstrated perfect enlightenment. To speak to fellow sufferers, to speak *for those that suffer* . . . it was (is) an impossible task.

Words do not bear the weight. Language can only point. West of India, near Ephesus in modern Turkey, the Greek philosopher Heraclitus knew: The god of Delphi, he supposedly said, neither speaks nor conceals, but gives a sign. Words indicate.

The Buddha came to the Deer Park at Benares. Legend again. There he enumerated the Four Noble Truths (*Arya-satya*): 1) All is suffering (*duhkha*, meaning the impermanence of existence and the unsatisfactory nature of that existence); 2) Craving—attachment—is the cause of suffering; 3) Craving can be "blown out"; 4) This is done by the Middle Way, the razor's edge, the noble Eightfold Path: right understanding, right speech, right action, right livelihood, right effort, right mindfulness, right concentration, right thought.

The noble Eightfold Path, the way (*dharma*) of the Buddha, was not enough for me.

The great and wise Buddha neglected the Ninth Way, for me the most important of all: *right blood pressure*. For me, and fifty million others in this country, there needs to be a *Ninefold Path*.

You who have some other chronic illness are welcome to a tenth, an eleventh, twelfth. . . .

Disease, my fellow suffers, is our special teacher and we sit at its feet. Chronic illness puts all practices to the test. Years of study, degrees and lineages, titles and blessings—which tend to fortify the ego-self—are like newspaper scraps blown about deserted city streets on a cold morning. We need to guard against Mara's endless tricks, the easy explanations. Such illusions distract us from the hard lessons of our diseases. Yet the sun shines and it is time to speak of dark things. The sun, said the ancient philosopher Diogenes, shines into the privies and is not defiled.

My ninefold path begins with those first weeks in the dialysis clinic. But the journey is circular. There are peaks, but also deep ravines, mist filled and dangerous. And then the traveler turns to survey the winding path behind . . . and, behold, sees only the sharp spires. Such is memory. So one must dig into those deep mysterious gorges.

It is thus a fragmented journey, a journey taken without steps. It is a path taken in the sky-blue dialysis chair where my blood flows through plastic tubes into a strange machine with beeps and buzzers and whirs and sirens . . . an incomprehensible machine that preserves my life.

# Part I

# Vlad the Impaled

# ☞ 1 ☜

# Abandon All Hope

(DANTE, INFERNO, CANTO 3)

Monday morning, September 14, 1998, still feeling the summer heat, I arrive at the dialysis clinic
before sunrise. For others it is a routine day, sipping their
morning coffee, driving to work . . . and I, too, once drove
to work in a factory. But this day I would trade for the
most dismal job. Today I am to enter dialysis.

For six years I've dreaded this moment. More accu-
rately, I've denied this moment, telling myself it would
never happen. When visiting my father on dialysis, I
would look away, not wishing to learn the mysteries of
the machine, perhaps in the irrational fear that too much
familiarity would consign me to his fate. He held out into
his fifties before dialysis. I'm forty-eight.

The clinic is a single storied sprawl, mostly metal
painted green and silver, with large almost wall-sized
windows, blinds closed, and a vaulted archway at the
entrance. Aseptic and severe, it overlooks a major highway. Countless times I've driven down this highway,
consciously not looking at the clinic, as if not seeing
would somehow spare me driving into its parking lot as
a patient. Not looking would somehow halt the little

deaths occurring in my kidneys. The most honest philosophers have said it: We really don't want to see, don't want to know.

I find a seat in the crowded waiting room. The majority of the patients my age are African-American males. For reasons not yet fully understood, twenty-five percent of the African-American population is hypertensive compared to fifteen percent of whites. Other patients are very old, an equal mix of male and female, black and white. Some are in wheelchairs. Many look sick: emaciated, stiff-legged, bruised, tired, and drained. "But I don't belong here! I'm an athlete: How many of you have run the Boston Marathon?" How stupid and egotistical to think such things, whispers mindfulness, even as I think them.

I glance at their forearms, searching for the oversized fistulas, where the artery has been surgically grafted onto a vein near the surface of the skin. This operation creates the access for the dialysis needles. There are two such needles, usually sixteen gauge (large bore), one arterial and the other venous, both inserted into the fistula. The needles are equipped with plastic butterfly wings to stabilize them on the skin. The blood flows from the arterial needle into the tubes and the machine, circulating back through the venous needle into the patient. The process has been explained to me many times. As if I could forget!

The waiting room is noisy for so early in the morning; lots of talk, laughter, stories from the weekend, then more laughter. Some of it sounds forced. But who can tell in this place?

∾

I should have started dialysis in May. April to be honest. I held out until September, suffering, causing my family to suffer. Denial, everyone says. Yet, denial seems too simple a term, concealing more than it illuminates. Perhaps it'll take this entire memoir to adequately treat denial. These handy labels are like fast food, quick but without lasting sustenance.

I do vividly recall feeling that if I could run every day, no matter what the blood numbers said, I didn't need dialysis. Prepared to collapse, I ignored the signs as best I could. Even that evening before the first treatment I ran three miles, still wondering if I should go the next morning. I ran hoping to escape the inevitable, but my steps were heavy and slow and tired. Maximum depression overwhelms many patients just before starting dialysis; some commit suicide. No doubt I felt anxiety, maybe fear, but also the determination I used to feel before beginning a long race. Maybe it was stubbornness? Maybe I'm just an ornery bastard who refuses to believe anyone? Or, maybe the runner's high, the famous endorphin rush, keeps depression at bay?

At last the waiting room is emptied. One by one the nurses escort patients into the clinic. A computer printed sign is taped to the door leading into the clinic. It warns patients not to enter by themselves, but to wait for their nurse. The warning is signed by the manager, the master of this small world, whom I shall call Big Daddy (the name given to him by the nurses themselves). I will come to know this clinic manager well—this Big Daddy.

I'm alone now in the antechamber. Have they forgotten? All week I'd been on the phone: to my nephrologist, the head nurse, other functionaries, meticulously preparing for this day. I am to begin slowly; the first treatment will last two hours. The next day I'll go two and a half, the day after three. Three days in a row, then a day off, then Friday. My "normal" schedule will be Monday, Wednesday, and Friday. But this first week will determine how well I "tolerate" dialysis. Some patients *never* tolerate dialysis; it never works and they die. The causes remain largely unknown. The first physician to use dialysis, the inventor of the first artificial kidney, Dr. Willem Kolff from the Netherlands, lost fifteen patients in 1944 before one survived treatment. A sixty-eight-year-old housewife, Sophia Schafstadt, survived until her renal function returned. Kolff had to deal with the fact that her son was an alleged Nazi sympathizer, and the Nazis had invaded his native Holland.

I sit there grasping the first volume of Gibbon's *The Decline and Fall of the Roman Empire*. I've made a pledge to read the entire thing; Gibbon will be my "dialysis book." Now I try to read, but the words are dim and vibrate. My heart is beating so fast that my hands shake. No doubt my blood pressure is surging. *Right blood pressure!* I smile grimly.

Finally a nurse comes and calls my name. Such formality. I'm the only person left! Later I learn that she's the wife of a doctor. Now she makes small talk, but I can't focus and don't know how to respond.

She weighs me, takes vital signs. It is as I'd guessed: My blood pressure is off the charts, one hundred and eighty over one hundred and two.

The clinic is large, about seven rows of sky-blue chairs with a dialysis machine per chair. Anywhere from twenty to thirty patients are dialyzed on the morning shift. I'm led to the front row, first chair. Overhead are televisions, three per row. I glance up; the morning news programs.

At this moment, however, television has never seemed so artificial and banal, news from another planet.

The dialysis machine stands about four feet tall and rests on tiny wheels. Clamped to its left side is an artificial kidney with my name stenciled on it. Officially it is called a dialyzer, a cylinder filled with membranous filters. Washing fluid, the dialysate, is pumped in and the membrane then filters out the molecules made up of waste products and toxins. The computerized machine is all lights and gauges with, I will learn soon enough, irritating buzzers and high-pitched sirens. The nest of blood-filled tubing is quite visible, clamped to the face of the machine so that it's easy to remove and replace for the next sufferer.

The nurse—Susan is the education nurse, hence she has a fledgling nurse alongside—gives me two injections of lidocaine, freezing the fistula. Then she inserts— "sticks"—the dialysis needles. I cannot look (I never look). I try to focus on the TV screen: Some happy newsperson is making gestures and smiling as she speaks, but there's no sound and she strikes me as quite ridiculous. Surprisingly, the needles go into my arm without pain. Susan then connects the tubing at the end of the needles to the machine. All the time she's talking to me, but to this day I cannot recall a word of the conversation, or whether I even answered. The pump, housed at the center of the machine, is a rotating block of metal around which a thick tube is strung. The rotation squeezes the blood through the tube, pumping it out of my body through the dialysis cycle.

My fistula is in the forearm of my right arm, mainly because I am left handed. Most others have theirs in the left arm. Therefore all the machines are left-handed, which means that the tubes leading from the needles to the machine are draped across my lap. The pump is turned on. Instantly the tubes become red . . . followed quickly by all the tubing in the machine . . . finally the kidney. I'm still not feeling anything strange; it's hard to believe my blood is now flowing outside my body.

I don't remember Susan's conversation. She talked for a long time. I do recall thinking of a new name for myself. Having fallen into another world, another life, I figured I'd require a new name that fit the circumstances. Back in the fifteenth century, the bloody-handed Count of Dracul was named Vlad the Impaler, Vlad Tsepesch. Count Vlad was so named for his grisly habit of spiking his enemies from the groin through the top of the head; hence, Vlad the Impaler (his son shared this particular talent and was called the Little Impaler).

Well, I laughed silently, as I am impaled with needles, I shall be called from this time on: Vlad the IMPALED.

Now should you be so inclined to deconstruct my new name, Vlad the Impaled (perhaps to serve the cause of psychoanalysis), you might see that within Impaled is PALE, which exactly describes me at the sight of those needles: I am im-PALE-d.

Two hours pass quickly. I try to read Gibbon's account of Roman military tactics. Not for the last time, do I contemplate the joys of kidney failure in the ancient world. In fact, the Romans used hot baths to treat people bloated with excess fluid (a symptom of renal failure, but also cardiac problems). The hot water caused the patient to sweat profusely and the skin acted as a toxin-diffusing membrane. My running, especially on extremely hot days, mimicked this procedure, but without the hot water. Needless to say, such "treatment" ultimately failed.

Most of the other patients are asleep. They were fairly loud for an hour or so, but now most are unconscious. Time on the machine goes by much quicker in that state. The television passes from program to program, news, talk shows, game shows. The world in a box.

Suddenly it's over and I'm walking out of the clinic, a bit light-headed and woozy but otherwise alive. The puncture wounds still bleed because of the heparin they injected to prevent the blood from clotting in the machine. The wounds begin to bleed more seriously as I drive out, and I'm forced to stop and apply pressure. I suddenly realize that I've been using the arm to shift gears in my jeep. Perhaps I'll have to sell it.

By the time I arrive home, the bandages are completely soaked. Once more I feel a mindless surge of panic. Finally the bleeding stops. I dare not take off the bandages, so I believe. Later, I learn to take them off in the late afternoon. The next morning the nurse chuckles as she removes the blood-encrusted mess. She explains the process to me, as if teaching a rather dull child. Don't worry, bleeding is normal due to the anticoagulant heparin. It will cease in less than an hour, silly boy! Despite my father, I'm still a dialysis innocent. Yet, the experience is invaluable—it is always a good thing when an academic is reminded of the depth of his ignorance.

Vlad the Impaled.

～

Looking for a bit of humor, I joke with friends when they ask why I waited so long before submitting to treatment, thus risking death. A philosophical experiment, I say. I hoped to gain a glimpse of the tunnel leading to the next world, of the light therein, or of some holy personage, or some guide. But I saw nothing except darkness, and there was no one to guide me. So now I'll finally read Gibbon and let the old Englishman be my guide. Few (if any) find this amusing.

I heard somewhere that Jorge Luis Borges got his first job in the Argentine National Library. He comes to work and sees everyone disappear into the stacks, not to reappear until five. So, the next day, he brings Volume One of Gibbon, and as time goes on reads the entire *Decline and Fall of the Roman Empire*. Borges claimed later that he would never have read the classic had it not been for the work ethic of Argentine librarians. I can say the same about dialysis.

The first week goes well enough. Everything is still new and strange: the nurses, the patients, the routine. We get weighed, our blood pressure is taken, our heart rate, our temperature. The needles are inserted. I think of it as Vlad getting impaled.

Since I don't look, the tubes seem to turn red instantaneously. Once circulating through the machine, the rate of blood flow is impossible to perceive. My own flow rate is 500 cc's per minute. It is still difficult to grasp that this is my blood.

Friday is the first three-hour session. It is still hard making small talk; when I do, it is only to introduce myself to the nurses and fellow patients. There's a deep urge to remain a stranger, to avoid the society of dialysis. The other patients most likely perceive this as arrogance, elitism, the stuck-up professor. And I question my own behavior. Perhaps they're right. Yet, I refuse to be sick. I will not give in. I will not "live" for dialysis. Somehow—perhaps the thought is irrational—by remaining apart I will preserve whatever vigor remains in my wasted body. Do I still think my kidneys will come back?

The nurses wear plastic shields over their faces, like clear, over-sized sun visors. They're continually washing their hands and using up those ubiquitous rubber surgical gloves. When dealing with patients they wear ankle-length white lab coats. In these times, blood can be a major weapons system.

I watch them, noting the fear-driven care, idly wondering if anyone has contemplated "the religious phenomenology of hemo-dialysis." Blood, of course, is immensely symbolic: the Savior's blood, ritualized in the Eucharist. But I'm thinking more along the lines of Exodus 24 where Moses takes the blood of the covenant sacrifice and splashes it all over the people of Israel. In Tarsus, Paul's hometown, the cult of Mithra dug a pit, placed the acolyte in it, then sacrificed a bull above, showering the acolyte with blood. There were many other such rituals no doubt. Blood is life. Religion "yokes" one to life (*religio*, in Latin means "re-yoke").

In our age, this ancient symbol of life has become also a dealer of death. Hence the protection. A reverse ritual, one might say.

Every Wednesday we get computer readouts from blood taken before treatment on Monday. This quickly becomes *my ritual*. The report is broken down into eleven categories: My weekly values are in the left-hand column; the "acceptable" values are in the right. Some are far too low, others far, far too high. It is like a weekly report card.

My first such blood report, representing my condition before beginning dialysis, was obviously in the realm of "corpse-like."

Serum creatinine, a waste product that comes from both meat protein and the normal wear and tear of muscles, was nearly sixteen—normal ranges from 0.5 to 1.5. Blood urea nitrogen (BUN), also produced from protein breakdown, but more closely related to diet than creatinine, was over two hundred—normal ranges about ten to twenty. Hematocrit, a measure of oxygen-carrying red blood cells, was twenty, when it should be forty or more, hardly enough to energize a squirrel.

Some things, such as potassium and phosphorus, can be controlled through diet. A dietician hands out the reports and informs us of those foods we need to avoid. When such elements fall beyond the acceptable values, we get a stern lecture from both the dietician and the physician. When good, we receive a stenciled "smiley-face" with the word "great" written beneath. The stencil comes in green or red, on rare occasions blue. It is like a blessing.

I laughed so hard my wounds popped open the first time I received a smiley-face. Yet, after a month, and despite my cynicism, I discovered that it worked. I was disappointed when I failed the blood exam, elated when I got my "great."

From big-mouthed professor to dull, silent child—intelligence and status are surely contextual.

≈ 2 ≈

# Limbo

They refer to it as a "dialysis honeymoon," these first weeks. I'm still an innocent, in a kind of Limbo. It is my time to read Gibbon.

I tell myself (and my family) that I'm feeling better. Food seems to have some appeal again, no longer like poison. Indeed, I learned that without kidneys the very stuff one needs to live quickly becomes so poisonous that the body evacuates it immediately. In the context of health, food is life-giving, in the context of illness it is poison. Again, a lesson in logic.

If I were one of those ancient Romans in Gibbon I would have died this month, despite the baths or the running. Bloated, without energy, stuffed with toxins, starving, my lungs might have filled with fluids and I would then suffocate, if I didn't starve first or die from a stroke or a heart attack. But here to the clinic I go . . . to live. Every week I wonder why.

"I go to die and you to live," said Socrates in the *Apology*. He'd just been condemned by the court in Athens. "But which of us has the happier prospect is unknown to anyone but God."

Today—a Wednesday, the first day of autumn—goes very badly in dialysis. My fistula is not yet "mature," they say. It is difficult getting the blood to flow at the prescribed rate. The nurses twist and jiggle the needles, trying to thread the artery properly. By now the lidocaine had worn off and I can feel every tiny pull and push.

Finally, they are forced to actually pull a needle out. There's a ten-minute wait while I hold the wound to stop the bleeding; then they stick me a third time. I try to remain outwardly composed but am betrayed by rising blood pressure and heart rate. And then my arm begins to spasm, and the machine goes off, beeping a high-pitched warning and flashing a red light, and for a moment I wonder if somehow I missed the sign that says: "Surrender all hope ye that enter here."

Big Daddy comes over and examines my arm. Now it's official. "Not mature," he pronounces.

"But I've had it since March," I protest.

He shakes his head and then makes a joke, which to this day I cannot remember.

Not mature. . . . Somehow I'm to blame for the sticking problems.

Yet, even after a mere two weeks, I'm beginning to learn that there are some nurses who seem gifted in the art of sticking. Others, no matter how dedicated, how diligent, are a threat to life and limb. There seems to be no rationalizing this gift. Some simply possess a sense, a feel for the needle in the vein. They sense exactly how much pressure to apply, how quickly to push the needle into the skin, where to insert it. Their talents are uncanny.

One of these artists of the needle is an older nurse, Momma Cass. She's been in dialysis for years, says she loves it. She's heavy and blonde and gentle and soothing. I relax whenever she approaches.

Then there's Vicki, with the most experience of all, who is consistently unable to stick my fistula. It frustrates her. She tries harder, and I get huge swellings as the needle pierces the vein and blood hemorrhages into the muscle. Hematomas, or "hema-tomatoes" as the joke goes. Now I like a joke as much as the next guy, but it takes time for me to laugh at these hema-tomatoes.

Momma Cass *never misses*. When I see her coming out to get me, I instantly relax, and perhaps, so too, the fistula. However, after a month she tells me that she's decided to change shifts (there are two other dialysis shifts: afternoon and evening) and wants to know if I will follow her. But I can't—childcare—and I realize suddenly how dependent I've become upon both machine and nurse.

Momma Cass is leaving me. Panic abruptly seizes hold. The dialysis honeymoon is over.

Yet, other patients have these kinds of problems, and much worse. Now I'm starting to notice. It took weeks for me to finally look about the clinic. Most of the others around me are old and very ill, suffering a multitude of ailments besides kidney failure. A few have that undeniable pallor of death; they're struggling with some life-threatening disease. Others are young, younger than me. One African-American girl can be no more than fourteen. I gaze at her and the Buddha's first Noble Truth, life is suffering, resonates.

It is easy to become overwhelmed, dragged down, by this sick house, this house of the nearly dead. Like Dostoyevsky in *House of the Dead*, where the prisoners are taking a group shower and the scene mutates into a scene from hell—naked bodies jammed together lost and confused and suffering—or like some frightful Hieronymus Bosch painting, the clinic threatens to slide into such a hell.

But I pull myself back. Surely it is exaggerating to think of the clinic in terms of Dostoyevsky's Russian prison. The officials are here to help me, to cleanse my blood, to bring me back from the edge. "You couldn't have felt very good," Big Daddy once said to me—we were discussing why it took me so long to submit to dialysis.

"No," I admit it, perhaps for the first time. "But I still ran," I add quickly.

"Well, don't you know that we can help?"

They can help, yes.

Yet, close your eyes and listen. Behind (or beneath) the nurses' chatter, the beeps and buzzers honking their warnings, one hears moans and gasps and cries and every imaginable sound of human distress. There is a veritable din of suffering.

And yet, patients call to one another, joke, tell stories, get into arguments, laugh like mad.

"I encourage laughter," says Big Daddy. He tells me this after *four attempts* on my abused arm.

"I hire people for their sense of humor, and the more perverted the better. You gotta laugh and joke in this place."

He goes off, needling a favorite patient and laughing uproariously.

Later a nurse confides in me: "During my interview here, the most important question Big Daddy asked was if I had a sense of humor."

"Do you?"

"Of course!" She gets angry. It takes her three needles to get me running, along with a huge hema-tomato.

"This, I take it," pointing at the ugly swelling, "is a joke?"

~

I arrive at the clinic at 6:25 on a Friday morning. Taking a seat, I fervently pray to whatever gods happen to be listening: "Let the nurse be Momma Cass!" Nothing in life seems as important.

They begin to collect the victims. Since I run for a mere three hours, I'm usually the last. Four hours go first. In a week, my physician, Dr. Jung,[1] will add an extra half hour to my treatment, which he bases upon a mysterious ratio designated by the symbols KT/V, a measure of dialysis effectiveness. The formula is calculated by a computer from blood drawn after treatment. K stands for the rate at which waste products are removed; T is the length of treatment; and V is the amount of water in the patient's body in relation to height, weight, and age. Mine was too low, hence the need for more dialysis.

Today there's an old, balding man in a wheelchair, dumped off by an open-bed truck from a nursing home near the clinic. He's been here since my first day, but up till now I haven't noticed him.

At last, he and I are the only two left in the waiting room. I still have a long list of gods to go through, praying for Momma Cass. The wait seems extra long, twenty minutes now. The old man begins to moan: "Oh why? Oh why oh why? Oh why? Oh why oh why?"

---

1 Not C. G. Jung, the Swiss psychologist and avatar of the New Age. Yet, C. G. Jung is the source. For six months before starting dialysis, I'd drive to University Hospital for a weekly appointment with "Dr. Jung." The attendant who operated the gate at patient parking would stop me ever time and ask my business. For several months I played the game and gave my renal physician's true name. One day, feeling irritated and depressed, I answered sarcastically: "Dr. Jung!" "Go on," he yawned. It became a game: I tried Dr. Freud, and that worked. Then Dr. Schweitzer. No problem. I might have pushed it to Dr. Einstein, but settled on Dr. Jung.

On and on, increasing in volume and then falling, like a wounded soldier on a battlefield without hope of rescue.

I try to concentrate on Gibbon. But even the entertaining crimes of the Emperor Commodus cannot compete with the old man in the wheelchair (later I learn his name is Danny).

Suddenly he shouts: "Why don't they come?"

And just as suddenly, in the very next breath, his tone becoming plaintive, he groans: "Son of a bitch! Son of a bitch . . . goddammit, goddammit!"

Then abruptly back to "Why oh why . . . ?"

And so it goes, like two people arguing: "Son of a bitch, goddammit . . . why oh why . . . OH WHY?"

Finally the charge nurse, an ex-navy corpsman I've grown to trust, comes and wheels him in, bidding me to follow.

The old man is still complaining. Some of the nurses laugh at him; others chide him for being a baby. Some of the patients ridicule him, but others are on his side: "You tell 'em Danny! Don't you take their shit!"

I think to myself, yes, a philosopher.

Some months later, I hear Danny, about two hours into treatment, begin to cry: "Oh please, get me off this machine! I can't stand it. Goddammit, get me off. Can't stand it."

A nurse tells him that he needs to run for another hour. He continues and she tells him to quiet down, that he's disturbing other patients. But he doesn't appear to hear.

"Oh please, oh please. Take me off."

I try hard to concentrate on Gibbon. The eighteenth century Englishman is talking about the slow, nearly invisible decline of the Roman Empire in the second century of this era. I read, "The form was still the same, but the animating health and vigour were fled."

I put the book on my lap, on top of the red tubes, and close my eyes.

~

After three weeks, despite on-going problems with sticking, I'm feeling better: eating, sleeping, participating more in the daily flow of life.

Now starting to get a feel for the depths of illness, I'm simply amazed to compare the present with just a month ago. The body possesses an incredible ability to adjust to even the deadliest conditions. And adjustment is so slow, so unconscious. One doesn't even think of oneself as sick. This is how I am, one says, and goes on.

Two months before treatment, I was reading new accounts of life in the most brutal of Stalin's labor camps. There were strong people in those camps, survivors one would guess, and yet they were crushed by the conditions. They seemed to gladly perish.

Others adapted to the unthinkable environment. Many suffered from a chronic illness. Surprisingly, some of these might have been considered weak, soft, terrified— yet they lived. Naturally, some of the strong survived too, and that's just the point. There's no generalizing. Who can tell beforehand? Some adjust to almost anything.

Most of the time, the victim of a creeping illness is simply unaware of the tiny continual adjustments. Perhaps at times, but dimly, does one sense the concessions to sickness, the compromises, the territory conceded inch by slow inch. "No, I don't want to do *that* anymore, don't *need* that . . ." Life adapts to the new conditions. And death, one begins to suspect, is another in a long line of adjustments, a far point on a continuum. I cannot lay claim to being fearless, and I certainly resented the creep-ing darkness. Yet as my life ebbed away, death seemed, well, natural. And, naturally, such thoughts oozed from a toxin-soaked brain.

One day, as the tubes turn red, I overhear nurses talk-ing about the millennium. At this moment, I decide to write this memoir and record those slow adjustments.

# ❦ 3 ❧

# Worthy Souls

(DANTE, INFERNO, CANTO 4)

For many patients, the cause of their kidney failure is their diabetes. Others share my illness, hypertension. Like me, they never found the Ninefold Path. The older people generally suffer from nonkidney related diseases. Some had strokes, vascular disease, or weak hearts.

At the beginning of treatment some patients engage in animated conversation, laughter, jokes—they flirt with the nurses—they even get into arguments that sound as if words will lead to blows. Much of the talk is difficult to follow. After an hour most are asleep or watching TV.

All of them are on disability thanks to the Social Security Amendments Bill of October 30, 1972. The final legislation determined that Medicare would cover all individuals with renal failure. Most patients depend upon public transportation to get to clinic, which sometimes they miss, or the vans miss them. Many were manual laborers before dialysis.

The two men sitting next to me worked on the railroad. Today their lives revolve around the dialysis clinic; they even wear tee shirts with the clinic logo.

Philip R. sits across from me. He's sixty, gray-haired, carries a fluid distended belly, and quickly becomes irritating. He badgers the nurses without mercy, although some appear flattered by his attention. He screams every time they stick him (in the leg). He argues constantly with another patient, Bill, who sits behind (neither is able to turn and face the other), threatening to "kick ass," which I find hilarious given that we're all half-dead, spiked and drained, and not going anywhere. He routinely propositions the nurses: "I feels I'm not long for this world; how 'bout having my baby, a little Philip R. to carry on my name?"

Yet, I soon learn that Philip R. has been on dialysis for eighteen years! He lost one transplant when he forgot to take his antirejection medicines on a trip. Poor, illiterate, addicted to TV, he thinks that all the doctors are stupid, "and don't know nothin'." This, by the way, is an opinion one constantly hears in many medical establishments. Once I suggested that after all those years of medical school they surely must have picked up "somethin'."

Philip R. calls for the nurses even when they're with other patients. Most say that they're busy. Still he insists and gets angry when they refuse.

A few, however, obviously enjoy the flirtation. They flutter over Philip, giggling, clucking, acting offended, shocked but obviously craving the attention. Sometimes they will flirt with him even when their patient's buzzer goes off (meaning that the pump stops, the blood ceases to circulate, clots develop). Yet they giggle and bounce around Philip, oblivious to the alarms, squirming at the attention like happy puppies. One, whom I shall call Peggy, is positively dangerous.

At times I sense a subterranean disdain among the nurses for the job. Most are Licensed Practical Nurses (not Registered Nurses, RNs, who must pass a more rigorous state board). Dialysis nursing does not entail the pressures of hospital nursing. Peggy, clucking and giggling, once told me that she couldn't take the hectic pace of hospital work. Here she gets to know the patients, she says, like Philip.

Often Philip R. will begin to moo like a cow, bark like a dog, or make incomprehensible noises, perhaps out of boredom, or to convince himself and others that he's still alive, more simply, still here. One's life here can easily slide into the most basic functions: eat, sleep, dialysis. One goes from treatment to treatment, suspended between illness and health, living a kind of marginal existence. Between treatments is the waiting, mere existing. Illness becomes an obsession; the body's basic functions become the whole of life. It seems as if Marx was thinking about dialysis patients when he wrote in 1844, "What is human becomes animal, what is animal becomes human."

After eighteen years it would surely seem that one has become a mere appendage of the machine (another Marxian thought). Only the basic animal functions belong to the human being. So one barks.

Who knows? He's just bored. Glued to that cursed chair for hours and dependent upon it for life would try the patience of a god.

Listening to my fellow patients, I wonder. Perhaps this is a room of potential buddhas, worthy souls preparing for the next round of incarnations, that will lead to taking up their fixed patch of earth earned through all the previous births and rebirths? The clinic is their field of enlightenment, the chair their bodhi tree.

I laugh to myself. Maybe I should test 'em? My fellow buddhas in training? Trot out a koan like: What is Buddha? Ten pounds of flax. Does a dog possess a buddha nature (that for Philip R.)? Mu! Such questions are called koans in Ch'an and Zen Buddhism. They are puzzles, arising first from Chinese legal disputes, designed to overcome conceptualizations and come to ultimate reality in which emptiness empties itself. The ego-self objectifies things—trees are trees *for me*—and in this process implies a independent, permanent self—trees always remain trees. But to negate that self by saying "no-self"—trees *are not* trees (my concept of tree)—smuggles in another form of self, "no-self." Therefore, the self of "no-self" must also be negated—trees are *really* trees (for themselves).

> A student asked Bodhidharma: "Please pacify my mind."
>
> Bodhidharma responded: "Bring forth your mind and I shall pacify it."
>
> Student: "Although I sought for it, I find it unattainable."
>
> Bodhidharma: "There, I have pacified your mind."

The negation of the negation is an affirmation; emptiness empties itself and reality stands forth.

Instead of cane beating for wrong answers, dialysis buddhas get an extra needle. Bad response, extra stick! Buddhism of the dialysis clinic.

Maybe I'm catching on to Big Daddy's sense of humor? Whatever the case, I decide to think of my fellow sufferers as buddhas, even Philip R. From now on in my mind they will be "the buddhas."

~

At times, when things go well, it appears I'm adjusting. Was it an unconscious, silent decision to go on in spite of the indignities? Samuel Beckett once phrased such a thought in this way: "You must go on, I can't go on, I'll go on." Unlike Beckett, I don't remember making the decision.

Treatment went better today, Friday. Big Daddy put me on and the blood flowed with the first set of sticks. It circulated through the machine so smoothly that the shrill siren remained silent for the entire three hours, a record. Most problems seem to occur on Mondays. My abused arm gets a two-day break over the weekend, and the puncture wounds heal. The scar tissue makes sticking more difficult. I appear to heal quickly.

"You're actually *too healthy*," says Big Daddy.

I offer a sincere apology for this heinous sin.

"You should be sorry. Don't heal so fast!" This reflects the clinic humor, which is vitally important to Big Daddy.

There's a story told by the Austrian (later Berkeley) philosopher, Paul K. Feyerabend, which comes to mind as Big Daddy waddles off, laughing. One day Feyerabend collapsed on a London street. He went to the English medical profession and endured the recommended battery of tests and "procedures," a word which can mean many things: You're gonna get cut, pierced, probed, jabbed, strapped, photographed—or more generally, robbed of your dignity. They made him feel terrible. The verdict: "You're in perfect health."

Feyerabend summarized his medical experience: "You are sick and you seek help, the medical profession makes you feel worse. Then they tell you you're all right."

But this Friday I'm able to concentrate on Gibbon and his account of the Parthians. The buddhas are strangely quiet.

~

With three weeks on dialysis, the toxin levels in my blood are falling. But I've experienced an interesting side effect. At night, usually around 1 or 2 a.m., I suddenly vault out of bed fully awake. *There's someone standing at the foot of my bed!* I can't identify him—I believe he's male—and the instant I come to full awareness he runs away. He's not a member of my family. The first time he appeared, I thought someone had broken into our house.

I raise my head to catch a glimpse and he's gone! He seems a denizen of that momentary state between drowsy wakefulness and full awakening, a borderlands person, a man of the in-between.

The fluid shifts, the filtration of toxins, the changes in body chemistry cause hallucinations, say the doctors. Slight chemical imbalances change perception. All hallucinations are accompanied by chemical imbalances, of course. Yet, I still wonder: Could it be something objective?

Perhaps if I don't move, he'll stay and talk to me? But no. He flees at the flicker of an eyelid. The visits become irregular. After a month, they cease. He never returns.

What should I make of this? How much are my sublime human abilities at the beck and call of chemical masters? Or, does the chemistry change come from the disturbance? What of free choice? What of moral perception, of the theological doctrine of sin?

~

Flo-Jo died during my first month on dialysis. She was only thirty-eight, a runner like me, but oh so much better and more accomplished. People are whispering about drugs. Yet, I glance around the clinic and note the hypertension cases, the high blood pressure that destroys kidneys, hearts, and other organs. I see the vascular disease. Such illnesses visit the generations. My own genes come from the southern Mediterranean, close to the northern coast of Africa. I went on dialysis at nearly the same age as my father. I don't know my family history in Sicily.

The day Flo-Jo died, I was, as usual, trying to read Gibbon. I came upon a passage in which Gibbon is quoting from the Roman historian Tacitus. Writing about the northern German tribes, Tacitus remarks that the Germans in their cold forests are longer-lived and healthier than the peoples of the Mediterranean, apparently holding up the Romans to scorn.

One must be careful reading the ancients, yet the passage seems synchronistic. We know that climate does not have a direct, Lamarckian influence upon genetics. Yet, pondering Tacitus, the blood draining from my body in an ironic vampire-like twist—drained to stay alive— it strikes me how much of my existence has become a struggle *against* my genetic inheritance.

This is the day Dr. Jung comes by and adds another half-hour to my treatment time. Now I must endure three-and-a-half hours of dialysis, Monday, Wednesday, and Friday.

Shortly, I come to see that this extra thirty minutes demonstrates the mysteries of "time." The hands of the clock never seem to move; they stop at nine-thirty (three hours) and refuse to budge. It is like time dilation in Einstein's Special Theory of Relativity—time and space are linked together. Time is measured differently in the coordinate system of the dialysis chair. Time stops after three hours on dialysis.

~

The philosopher Martin Heidegger was obsessed with a quote from van Gogh's letters: "I feel with all my strength that the history of human beings is precisely as it is in the case of wheat: If one is not put on earth in order to blossom, then one ends up getting milled in order to make bread."

On dialysis one does both. One's arm is milled into bread by the needles; one suffers the many side effects. Yet, I do feel better, and so the possibility to blossom is not lost.

# ❧ 4 ❧

# To Rome

(DANTE, INFERNO, CANTO 1)

They're having problems with my dry weight, knowing how much excess fluid to take off during each treatment. Running five to six miles daily throws them off. On hot days, I lose extra fluid from sweating—the old Roman treatment—which skews their measures.

I can hardly call what I do every afternoon "running." My hematocrit is still low, meaning I possess barely enough red blood cells to carry the required oxygen to starved muscles. Memory says I should be going faster and farther. But my legs move like rusty bolts. Even my dog and running partner, Misha, a hundred pound malamute, seems to notice. Yet, he's quite happy to go slower. It gives him the chance to stop at every tree and pee, which I've come to envy.

Today—a beautifully blue and bright early October Friday—is another bad session. Vicki sticks me, pushing the needles in without difficulty. But then, half way through treatment, the damned siren goes off, the red light starts to blink, and the pump stops. The fistula begins to spasm. I feel the wrenching halt of the circulation.

The nurses hover over me. Someone—maybe it's the corpsman but I'm not looking—begins to jiggle the needles. Then he actually flips them over, squeezing their green plastic butterfly wings to clear the flesh and rotate the needle.

"The needle must be hittin' the wall of the vein" is the verdict. Since the lidocane has worn off, the maneuver sends me into the upper heavens where the suffering saints have their abode.

The siren-sounding buzzer continues to protest. The pump remains motionless.

Now a clot develops in the machine and they hurry to clamp off the access lest the clot make its way there. Then they dismantle the many yards of tubing and toss it into a red garbage can marked "biohazard." My blood in those tubes is now "biohazard."

Not to worry, they tell me.

Meanwhile, Philip R. is vigorously trying to get a nurse's attention, not Peggy but another named Madonna. He tells her a lewd joke.

Finally they get me running again. They've retubed the entire machine to rid it of clots. Madonna takes my blood pressure. It's very high. She sighs . . . and then turns to giggle at Philip.

I go back to Gibbon and read his account of the Emperor Julian. Now, it seems, I feel a deeper empathy for lost causes.

At last the session is over and I'm free for two days. I step outside the clinic into the lovely weather. Yet, I'll be back here Monday, and possibly every Monday for the rest of my life. The thought plunges me into an overwhelming sadness.

On Monday we start all over. More trouble too.

It's Vicki, the most experienced nurse—she sticks me and apparently misses the vein completely. Instantly my arm swells—a hema-tomato. She tries again. No luck.

The corpsman gives it a shot, then Big Daddy. About fif-teen minutes into the session I'm sitting with four wounds and no dialysis.

"You'll have to go home and come back tomorrow," says Big Daddy. "You're not teaching today, right?"

"Yeah, I'm on sabbatical for the fall semester." Or should I say at a witch's Sabbath? I'm supposed to be researching and writing, not serving as a pincushion.

"Your fistula is curvy. You have curvy veins. Hard to stick."

"Oh, my veins are non-Euclidean?" I joke.

No one laughs.

Momma Cass is on vacation. Susan can stick me without problems, but it's her day off. Big Daddy says that it's clinic policy that everybody be able to stick every-body. It's probably a good idea in theory, but in reality it simply doesn't work. I'm at the mercy of people's work schedules, not only the machine.

I return Tuesday and the corpsman gets the needles in. I still run lousy.

Every day this week there's trouble with my fistula. They miss or go right through the vein. I am rewarded with a hema-tomato. On Friday, Nurse Vicki pulls out the second failed needle. I hold gauze over the wound, wait-ing for it to clot so she can stick me again. But she gave me heparin to prevent clotting, so I bleed . . .

After ten minutes, she peeks under the gauze. Blood squirts out and shoots halfway across the room! Vicki jumps back, dodging the deadly stream (all blood is deadly in clinic). The gauze instantly turns red and soggy. She gives me more, careful not to touch any blood.

*Finally* the bleeding stops and she inserts another needle. This one works even though the flow is still poor. Vicki shrugs and goes off to clean up the floor.

While all this unfolds, the buddhas across from me get into a very unbuddhist argument over the burning question: "Who is the Man?" Perhaps because of recent loss of blood, my faculties are too dull to grasp the full implications of the question. But it is taken very seriously. Again, I would guess that had they been able to leap out of their chairs, the argument would have erupted into a brawl, although I doubt anyone could do real damage given our weakened conditions. Nonetheless, the argument goes on for a long time, to the very end of treatment. No naps today.

The very next session, a Monday, the buddhas get into another shouting match, this time over the merits of various gambling boats on the river. Surprisingly, they ask me for my views, and I sheepishly tell them that I've never visited the boats, confirming their suspicions—I *am* strange.

Yet I'm happy today, no tomatoes. Vicki gets me with her first try and the blood flows at the required rate for the full three-and-a-half hours. I have the rare opportunity to actually concentrate on Gibbon, in this instance his account of the Arian Heresy. It is quite good, and I find myself silently cheering Gibbon's quiet but deep skepticism, and his good sense.

Reading, too, is a problem. My eyes blur after a short time. It is increasingly difficult to focus on the page. Once again it's the drastic fluid shifts, sometimes eight or more pounds at a time, that cause the troubles. Dr. Jung refers me to another specialist for my eyes. Medical care is becoming a full time occupation.

∼

Nurse Susan is a fundamentalist Christian, but she's very reticent about it; she doesn't seem to proselytize in the clinic and she's nice and gentle to me even though I think she's a bit frightened of me, a professor who has taught courses on the historical Jesus. In my language, the historian's dialect, she's a follower of the *Christos*, which is the Greek translation of the Hebrew term, Messiah, meaning in Hebrew "anointed"—what I would call a *Christophoros*, "Christ-bearer," the term perhaps used first by Ignatius of Antioch. Some professors who teach the course will ask their students on the first day: What religion was Jesus? Answers range from Protestant to Catholic; many say Christian. No, says the professor, he was a Jew. I'm tempted to ask her, but she's the one with the needles.

Over the weekend, she went to a revival. An important revivalist was in town. There were visions, healings, speaking in tongues, exorcism of demons, encounters with Jesus himself and, most significantly, "getting your wings." Susan got hers.

I look real hard but can't see her wings. Perhaps it's my dialysis-corrupted vision. As the blood flows I amuse myself by making up bad jokes about spiritual wings and bodies, and demons. Ancient demons have become chemicals. The machine casts them out.

Philip R. teases her about her wings, although I'm not too sure that he doesn't take them literally. But since I've acquired the reputation as a reader, she quietly presents me with a catalogue of her favorite books, titles like *Make Jesus Proud of You*, *The World Didn't Happen By Chance* (this against Darwin), *Your Angel* (we all have one; mine surely left town long ago), and of course numerous WWJD (What Would Jesus Do) artifacts. I experience the sudden urge to joke with her: WWJD? I gratefully accept the catalogue. It's called witnessing and now I see that she does proselytize. Quietly.

The buddhas and nurses are amazed by the sheer size of Gibbon. I tell them that there are two more volumes of equal or greater length (this being the Modern Library Edition).

Jake, an old and frail African-American sitting beside me, develops a running joke, for which I'm extremely grateful. Almost every day for three months, he asks: "Has Rome fallen yet?" And he roars with laughter.

Each time I answer: "Something as big as Rome takes a long time to fall. Not till volume three."

It never fails. Both of us laugh like madmen.

On Wednesday a doctor makes the rounds, checking every patient. Generally it's a different doctor every week. One of them, white-haired and looking like he should be captaining a yacht, comes by today and asks me what I'm reading.

"Gibbon."

"Gibbon?"

"Yeah. *The Decline and Fall of the Roman Empire* . . ." I hesitate. He looks puzzled.

"It's a classic. . . ." I don't know what to say, my wit seems to have drained away with my blood.

"I *know* it's a classic!" he says, sounding offended. "I prefer smaller books."

# ~ 5 ~

# A Babel of Despair

(DANTE, INFERNO, CANTO 6)

Dogen says deliverance means freeing oneself from long-winded discussion of doctrines and dogmas, and finding enlightenment in the mundane acts of everyday living.

Dogen was a thirteenth century Japanese Zen Buddhist philosopher who visited China as a young man. At his arrival in China, he met an old monk from a Zen monastery. The old monk was a cook who obviously preferred cooking to monastic practice. Dogen asked him why he didn't devote himself to meditation or a koan.

The old monk answered him: "My good fellow from a foreign land, you do not know what practice means, nor do you yet understand words or scriptures."

And Dogen realized that cooking had become the old man's meditation, his path.

Why not dialysis? It could become my meditation.

These Zen stories are very nice and motivational, but the reality of the clinic does not easily cook enlightenment. Rather, what simmers is depression, at times even despair.

"Depression" is one of those words like "denial." It may well be a detour from the long and difficult path of thinking.

The instant I complain—actually I hardly complained, I simply looked sad one day and said I felt down—they start lining up. First was the social worker. She says I need to immediately tell her of *any* problems. Why don't I listen to music while on the machine? Watch TV? Eat something? Chew on ice? Reading, a solitary act, breeds depression.

I make a terrible mistake by telling her what I'm thinking.

"I want to *think* about my illness," I say, "question the dumb fate of genetics, examine the deeper, religious issues of personal suffering, of suffering in general, of evil in the world. I want to ponder these universal questions even if they may be unsolvable, like the Buddha—sickness, old age, death. I cannot take your easy cures. I'm sick of the dictatorship of well being without contrary voices, like those smug smiles that fill the TV screens, the self-help experts who quickly leap over the darker chasms without honestly peering down and wondering. This savior-ridden, therapy-mad culture will simply not do!"

What an outburst! I immediately regret it, for the social worker pulls out a printed card, which reads: "Symptoms of Depression." And I'm faced with a battery of questions: Do I regress? Exhibit periods of noncompliance? Am I hostile, even to loved ones? Do I feel hopelessness? She reads as if from a shopping list. Do I experience insomnia? Fatigue? Lack of interest in sex (a big one in this culture!)? Am I resentful?

And so what if I am? If I do? Do I need to be physically sick to feel such things? But I shut my big mouth, having learned my lesson.

She hurries off. The verdict is that I require counseling.

But look at the buddhas. Their constant flirting with the nurses seems like verbal compensation for what kidney failure does to the libido. Sometimes I imagine that their sexual obsessions are a frightened cry against the creeping death, sneaking up behind us, coming closer every day. We are grabbing frantically for a little bit of life.

I've felt it, this gradual loss of interest in everyday activities, those things we take for granted. People, relationships, sex . . . all demand far too much energy for the kidney failures. And watching life flow past, like a disinterested spectator, I laugh at all the expended energy, the breathless anticipation, anxiety. It all seems absurd, ending, as I know it does in this darkness, this entropy.

Nothing, it now seems, can adequately describe this gradual sinking into the depths. Sex, for example, no longer exercises its former claims within my toxin-filled body. Naturally this loss frightens and saddens me, but it also makes me aware of the culture's use of this function, how sex-crazed advertising has become. In the summer before dialysis, when very sick and semiconscious of the libido's destruction, I often laughed, seeing clearly, perhaps for the first time, how the sexual drive is truly and thoroughly manipulated.

Watching television from the dialysis chair, I recall Prince Siddhartha's early life in his father's palace when every whim was instantly gratified, every wish fulfilled. He lived in paradise and still felt that something was missing (this is legend naturally). Desire is *never fulfilled* but begets further desires, which grow beyond any possibility of fulfillment. Thus we are cursed with craving and restlessness. *There is no self-fulfillment through indulgence.*

Ruefully, I wonder if kidney failure has removed me from the wheel. Slow death gives a different perspective on life. It is my perspective. I'm sure there are many, many others. Like Nietzsche. I think of what Nietzsche wrote:

> In a certain state it is indecent to go on living. To vegetate on in cowardly dependence on physicians and medication after the meaning of life, the *right* to life, has been lost ought to entail the profound contempt for society—death . . . with a clear head and with joyfulness, consummated in the midst of children and witnesses.

I could throw all of this at the social worker when she comes around again. Maybe it's time to refuse treatment, to leave with a clear head, not in the midst of the almost-dead, but with children.

I have three children: sixteen, eleven, and five. This slow fizzle of life is devastating to them. My eleven-year-old, Sophia, seems to take it the hardest. She suffers anxiety attacks; she, too, is sick, she says. Now she's dizzy. Is her blood pressure too high? Will she stop breathing in her sleep? Will she die young? Why doesn't Dad play with her like he used to? Will he ever be happy again?

So *when* is the right time to die? Nietzsche doesn't say. And among children? Among one's own children? Generalizations begin to sound ridiculous as my blood fills those tubes.

These things hurt worse than the needles. I'd gladly endure a hundred sticks rather than that frightened expression on my daughter's face, or the gloom that haunts Armine, my wife. Rather isolation, to die alone without dragging others down into the pit.

~

"You're experiencing the usual depression that comes with kidney failure and dialysis." Thus spake Dr. Jung. He's sitting comfortably behind his desk, talking to me within the sanctuary of his private Medical School office. My wife, a nurse employed with this same hospital, tells me that I should feel honored. I'm being treated like a VIP.

He's seen it many times before, depression due to a chronic illness.

Dr. Jung is very gentle and reassuring; a large man my age, he wears a well-trimmed beard and a jovial smile. In the course of our discussion (actually, his sermon), I learn that dialysis will never bring my toxins down to anything near normal. It makes sense: Normal kidneys function around the clock (though they tend to sleep with the rest of the body), seven days a week.

My artificial treatment is three-and-a-half hours, three days a week. I'd have to be constantly on the machine, but even then the toxins could not be brought down to "normal." For all of our technical expertise, we can't duplicate Dame Nature (or YHWH—the original Hebrew spelling of Yahweh, or Jehovah, without the vowels, as it occurs in ancient sources—if you prefer).

Oh, improvements are on the way, he assures me.

Ah, there's been a great deal written about progress, I respond, questioning how we measure it without assuming what we want to measure. Where is the fulcrum to make such a value judgment? Take your drugs. There's always some side-effect, sometimes worse than the original illness the drug is designed to treat.

My arguments are post-treatment depression, he says. Perhaps I need a therapist. However, Dr. Jung does say that he'll put in a word for me at the clinic so that I might be spared those nurses who miss the vein and cause me extra suffering. Still there's POLICY, he warns, every nurse sticks every patient.

But maybe I do need a therapist. . . .

With that I'm dismissed.

"How are you feeling?" Every Wednesday the doctor making the rounds asks the same question. How the hell would you feel stuck to this machine? Why can't I resent the instrument that preserves my life?

"Oh, just fine."

He reads my chart and then nods, smiling. It's the doctor who thinks Gibbon is too long. Yes, they are making me feel better, and I'm alive. I thank him and smile back.

It's all a form of therapy, from beginning to end, physical and psychological, the doctors and the social workers, the nurses, even Big Daddy. Give me a medieval priest!

There's a late entry in one of Franz Kafka's diaries that abbreviates my feeling: "for the last time, psychology."

This is rather comical. Just now, calling out for a medieval priest, up pops a modern Jew. . . .

# ⪻ 6 ⪼

# Chaos

(Dante, Inferno, Canto 12)

L ate October, the weather is still mild and bright, colors in the trees. Dying leaves are beautiful. I step outside the clinic, inhale deeply and try to appreciate the simple joy of a fine day. At times I succeed. Yet it is sad when the memories of other Octobers return.

Every morning at five, before going to clinic, I read half an hour of Jewish philosophers and rabbis. They're wrestling with the problem of a God who is Lord of History, all-powerful, all-good, and the obscenity of the Shoah, the Nazi genocide. At best, God seems irrelevant in the presence of an Auschwitz where a million children were murdered.

On mornings such as this, fresh from dialysis, I feel these issues deeply. Why this terrible suffering? Any suffering? What could we learn from the suffering of children that an infinite mind could teach us by some other, less frightful means? I've been teaching for nearly twenty years; one adopts various methods, different approaches, and yet one knows that there are many, many others. Use many metaphors, says Nietzsche, repeat yourself often, for you never know what will be effective with different people. Surely God is a better teacher than what history seems to show? Perhaps Nietzsche was right: He's dead.

Then I happen upon this story:

One night in Auschwitz, a group of Jews put God on trial and found Him guilty of permitting the obscenity of the camps. They condemned God to death for this unspeakable crime. When the trial was over, the presiding rabbi announced that it was time for evening prayer.

On the other hand, I read in the Hasidim about an idea that sounds quite Buddhist: Suffering, they say in regard to the camps, brings one out of the personal ego and closer to the divine. Thus it is necessary for the cosmos.

Yet, I find myself in a constant struggle *not to become my illness*, not to let it rule me. There is always the danger that the ego actually becomes inflated, that I become the suffering and extract a perverse pride and self-importance from it. I see this happen in my fellow patients—their favorite subject is themselves, obsessively.

So I refuse to quit running, though it is humiliating to run at the speed of grass growing. Glancing at the other patients in clinic, I tell myself *I am not one of them.* And yet this very desire is also ego enforcing. So I struggle with attachment to health and to illness. Sometimes I think of myself as a "marginal person." The psychologists might call it denial. But then, Dostoevsky wrote in *Notes from the Underground* that people pride themselves on their diseases. I'd rather laugh and remain in denial.

∼

Dr. Jung blesses me with another audience. He confides in me (perhaps it's still therapy) that there's a lot the medical profession doesn't know about renal failure (and he's one of the top guys in the field).

A few doctors are not even certain of the causal chain: whether the high blood pressure is the cause or the result of kidney destruction. Besides excreting waste products, kidneys produce substances such as renin and angiotensin, which may regulate blood pressure. As the kidneys die, blood flow into them decreases, and the kidneys secrete more renin, which tends to elevate blood pressure. Physicians call this chain of events "secondary hypertension" (primary hypertension is the inherited condition that destroyed my kidneys). Fewer than five percent of people who have high blood pressure suffer from secondary hypertension in which kidney failure was the cause. And yet, I wonder.

Even after my blood pressure was under control, in 1992, my kidneys still continued to decline. The cause had been removed, yet the effect continued as if on its own. And now, in the final stages of renal failure, my blood pressure resists the medications—"Your kidneys are fighting us," says the charge nurse, as if my kidneys were a foreign country carrying out terrorist acts.

Then Dr. Jung lets slip a rule of thumb: If fifty percent of kidney function is lost, total failure results, no matter what the treatment. I came to him with sixty percent. He gave me reason for hope—"You're not your father. . . ." Therapy? Please, no more psychology.

I describe to him as best I can the mathematics of chaos theory and complexity. I had begun to study these subjects and was able to solve the simplest equations until the toxins overwhelmed my beaner. This sounds like the phenomenon of "lock-in," I tell him. In complex, self-contained systems, processes reaching a certain limit seem to reinforce themselves and carry on toward some terminus. Order, on the other hand, may emerge spontaneously out of chaos.

All this is far too theoretical and abstract for medicine. Dr. Jung tells me, somewhat apologetically, that medicine is as much art as science.

I walk out of the university medical center, a very familiar place by now, into a lovely October afternoon. Every breath, moment of life, every glorious color of every leaf, becomes transfigured into glorious works of art.

~

At first glance, Nurse Vicki looks rather mean and perpetually angry, and she does try to act gruff and hard. Yet she is one of the most caring people in the clinic. She's worked here the longest. It's a shame she can't stick me.

Today Nurse Vicki is telling me about a former patient from many years ago. The poor guy suffered a stroke on the machine. When he returned from the hospital, all he could say was "yeah" and "damn." The nurses would play games with him. Did he like Nurse so-and-so? "Yeah." How about other patients? "Yeah, yeah." How about the clinic manager? "Damn. Damn."

As she tells the story, she sticks my arm . . . and misses. Now I'm the proud owner of a brand new hema-tomato. This time I lose my composure and shout, "Fuck!"

Vicki looks startled. She's never heard me use profanity. She looks offended and hurt.

"Sorry. I'm writing rap lyrics. A rap song about the clinic."

She doesn't laugh. Instead she gets help. It takes three nurses, all twisting and pushing, to get the needles in and my blood flowing. But it doesn't flow at the prescribed rate no matter how much they pull and twist.

Big Daddy is called. He gives my arm a thorough examination.

"Your fistula is not maturing," he pronounces like some judge in a court trial.

"But there're a few nurses—like Momma Cass—who've *never* had problems sticking me. Can't you just allow the Tony experts?"

"Nope. The problem's your arm. Everyone ought to be able to stick you."

"But people are different . . ."

"Nope. It's policy."

"Ah, policy." Policy says nobody's different.

He frowns, obviously in deep thought. "We'll have to make an appointment in radiology for a *fistulogram*."

"A what?"

"A fistulogram. They inject dye into your arm and x-ray it. They'll examine your fistula on screen. Probably some collateral veins need to be tied off. Maybe they'll do some *reaming* to open the artery." He laughs at this.

"Are you sure it's my arm and not your methods?" I protest. "Maybe you need to do an in-service on Tony sticking?"

"Oh no," he assures me. "It's you. And we have POLICY."

I try to quickly write rap lyrics about *policy*.

Dr. Jung is not happy about this development. But the clinic is a privately run business—the social worker spilled the beans—which means that his doctoral clout is limited. Policy rules. No exceptions.

On Wednesday, when we get the computer pages with our blood numbers, I call for the manager.

Big Daddy comes over and I show him the paper.

"This is my report. Go look at Philip R.'s, or any other patient's. They change week to week."

"So?"

"So they're not the same week to week, nor are they the same patient to patient. Why should policy be so static?"

"There'd be chaos," he says.

"Ah, but order arises spontaneously from chaos."

"What?"

"Never mind. Do I really need this fistulogram thing?"

"Yup."

At that moment my arm begins to spasm and the machine alarms. Today my blood pressure was elevated, and now it ascends to 160/100.

"See there." He walks away shaking his head.

Vicki comes over and says: "You're a hard stick."

"And a difficult person," I add. We both laugh.

The same day I start the second volume of Gibbon. He's discussing the Christians burning the great library of Alexandria. Surely the empty shelves, he sighs, must have brought a tear to the eye of those whose minds were not totally darkened by the fanaticism of religion. Or policy, I mutter aloud. Fortunately, no one hears.

As I read this passage, Jake asks: "Is Rome still fallin'?" He laughs very hard. The daily joke, obviously high wit.

I smile back and nod. "Yup, still fallin'. Volume two. It takes a long time."

*Part II*

Die Now, Diagoras

# But Be Still

(DANTE, INFERNO CANTO 26)

Today, Friday, is the day before Halloween. The nurses and some of the clerical staff dress up in costumes and parade around the clinic, weaving in and out between the rows of chairs. There are witches, cowboys and cowgirls, clowns, but nothing very original, not like the kids who come to the door. Although everyone wore masks, I identify each person without much trouble.

The patients love it. I cannot recall adults dressing up for Halloween when I was young. Nonetheless, I laugh and thank them for the effort.

In this part of the country, some people call Halloween the devil's holiday. A few nurses share this belief and were conspicuously absent from the parade of demons.

Once again, I make the mistake of speaking out: No, Halloween is hardly the devil's holiday but All Hallows Eve, the night before November First, All Saints Day, an old Church holiday.

"What Church?" Susan the fundamentalist asked.

"Uh, *the* Church . . . "

"*What* Church?"

"Oh . . . the *Catholic* Church." I must look puzzled.

Then I realize: Many of them believe that Catholics are not Christians! Susan abruptly discovers that her presence is urgently needed elsewhere in the clinic.

I'd heard such nonsense previously, from students. The statement always leaves me speechless. Apparently this is the considered opinion of some local Protestant clergy.

Once, I explained to a nurse that according to pious legend, Martin Luther, a *Catholic priest*, nailed his ninety-five theses to the Church door at Wittenberg on this day, All Hallows Eve. None of this, Luther or my protests, made the slightest impression. Halloween is the devil's holiday; Catholics are not Christians.

Nearing the end of treatment, I'm feeling light-headed, drained, washed-out—I can no longer focus on the pages where Alaric is marching upon Rome. Drastic fluid shifts make the outside world break apart and flow away; solids pass into fluids, finally into a blur of gas and vapor.

An old Zen poem seems to summarize the feeling:

> I awoke from a dream
>
> and realized I awoke into
>
> another dream.
>
> Reality exists beyond my vision.

~

The access is still not working properly and I've heard nothing from Dr. Jung or the mysterious radiology. Today, there are three wounds in my access. The nurse, the one

I name Peggy, talking about recipes with another nurse, stuck right through the fistula with her first try. A frightful bruise, a hema-tomato, develops immediately. Then the arm begins to spasm. Meanwhile Peggy is now prancing and giggling in front of Philip R.; she ignores the blinking red light and shrill buzzer. Philip R. is telling her how sexy she is.

I'm more afraid than angry. The corpsman comes to the rescue.

~

Detachment!

Despite everything I know about mindfulness meditation, today I'm straining (interesting irony) to remain calm as Madonna inserts the needles. I try everything: breathing, meditation, the TV, even sleep. Momma Cass never has a problem, the corpsman is good, so too the head nurse, Big Daddy, and the other charge nurse named Bart. If I can relax, detach myself from the proceedings, sticking will not be a problem. But when the Holy Five are not about and the deadly majority descends upon me, I break into a fear-laced sweat.

It's not them. It's my arm. It's my attitude—altitude, I prefer, since altitude describes my physical and mental state when they miss or go through the fistula. But policy says everybody sticks everybody, no matter what the altitude.

Today Madonna needs four needles to get me going. She's talking to another nurse when she removes them at the end of treatment, and she tears the skin. It seems to me that I bleed forever. My shirt is soaked as if I've been in battle.

When Willem Kolff first began dialyzing people in the 1940's, he simply introduced his needles into veins and arteries. This usually meant that the number of treatments was limited, since new sites had to found every time and vessels were quickly used up.

Once, probably his ninth dialysis, he injected the needle into the patient's femoral artery through the groin. After it was removed, the wound continued to bleed until finally a surgeon was called to close it on the operating table. I've told students that history does not repeat itself, but now I begin to wonder.

I sit for an extra ten minutes and finally the wounds stop leaking. Meanwhile, I finish the march on Rome with Alaric. It took an exceedingly long time.

Rome is still falling, I tell Jake.

~

Big Daddy tells me that he's made the appointment for my fistulogram. It's set for Wednesday at 8 a.m., at the University Medical Center, in radiology on the second floor. Dialysis must be rescheduled (again!). This causes some problems in clinic, and Big Daddy is none too happy, although the whole thing is his doing.

On that Tuesday, I get a call from radiology. They can't take me at 8 a.m. tomorrow, how about 1 p.m.? I agree. What choice do I have?

A few hours later another call. How about 2 p.m.? Okay.

Late afternoon and the phone rings again. Radiology on the line: They can't do it tomorrow, or Thursday. How about Friday at 1 p.m.? I thank them.

Next day in clinic, I'm feeling down. It took three sticks and still I'm not running at full flow. The fistula spasms often; the machine flashes and beeps. The nurses and buddhas are no help; they're watching *Oprah*.

The social worker comes around and pulls up a stool. She tells me that there are "degrees of depression."

"No absolute depression?"

She frowns. Obviously, the toxins are cooking my brain.

"What is my degree?"

"Moderate."

"So I have a master's degree in depression? Do you have one in social work?"

She ignores this bad humor. "Radiology," she says, changing the subject, "will be a simple procedure. You've nothing to worry about."

"I'm glad."

"I'm glad too." And she's on to the next victim . . . uh, patient.

That evening, browsing a bookstore, I see a Zen title, *Open Mouth, Already a Mistake*. A perfect phrase for therapy. Next time they ask me how I'm feeling, I'll apologize for not speaking and then say: "Open mouth, already a mistake."

On dialysis, there could be an additional phrase: "Closed eyes, already asleep."

# ⚜ 8 ⚜

# New Torments

(DANTE, INFERNO, CANTO 6)

Friday, November 6, the day Newt Gingrich stepped down as Speaker of the House, I step into radiology. The news about Newt, the ongoing Clinton scandal, Washington politics—all of it seems unreal, an imposition, not worth thinking about. My reality is shrinking daily. Today my world is the medical center.

Simple procedures may be "simple" from the perspective of the medical profession, but for me, they are like Kafka's trial: Something is about to happen to me, I know not what, only that I'm guilty of something. They're doing things; I don't know what those "things" are.

Radiology looks like a high-tech version of Frankenstein's laboratory. Screens, computers, massive cameras, hundreds of incomprehensible gadgets, and at the center of the room is a menacing steel table, which brings to mind the word "dissection."

I'm ordered to take off my street clothes. The radiology nurse hands over one of those ridiculous hospital gown that ties in the back. I'm not up to that task, alas. She tells me to lie flat on the table (which is freezing), and then she straps me down so tightly that I can't move a muscle. My offending arm is strapped down onto a separate plate, which is hinged to the main table.

Meanwhile, nurses and techs bustle about the room, occupied by many mysterious tasks. I think there are five people in the room, but I can't be sure. They place a blood-pressure cuff on my fistula arm, something the vascular surgeon told me *never to do*. The wounds from this morning are still bandaged. They take the bandages off and I experience a moment of panic, afraid it will begin to spurt blood. Then another damned needle is inserted between the two wounds from the morning. I thought I got off luckily with two sticks; now it's three. Radioactive dye is pumped. The dye burns like fire, a little piece they left out of the description of "simple procedures." But all this is preliminary to the heart of the procedure: They inflate the cuff until my arm feels as if it'll explode!

Now they all exit, leaving me alone with the gigantic automatic camera that hovers like some metal, flesh-eating insect. The motors whir; it moves over me, actually pressing me down with its lens. I hear other noises, beeps and whirs of different pitch and tone. Twisting my head, I see that the screens are alight, and those tangles, what seem to be branches and vines, are actually my arteries and veins.

The cuff deflates and I'm given a respite. Then they begin again as if to extract a confession. But it is the screen that must confess, and this information I cannot translate. Five times they repeat this "simple procedure."

Two hours pass. I'm stiff and cramping, still bolted down and helpless. The particular odor of terror fills the room; I smell so bad I can hardly stand it. No wonder they cleared out.

At last, they emerge from hiding. The radiologist is there, looking rather bored. The others begin the cleaning process. I'll never know how many assisted. In a flat tone, the radiologist says that the fistula *looks perfectly fine*—no clots, no blockage, no blood drained away by subsidiary veins. He doesn't understand what the problem could be. My access ought to be working perfectly.

I protest weakly. Still tied down, however, I try not to sound argumentative. But he doesn't listen. Next patient!

*My fistula ought to be working. . . .*

That Monday one of the nurses, a tall, black woman named Ramona, asks me why I have "such a shitty access."

"Why, oh why . . . ?"

～

The other nurses act surprised when I tell them that radiology pronounced my arm fit to stick. Big Daddy seems to doubt my word. The toxins cause confusion, so I probably didn't hear correctly, he says. Later, the report vindicates me. I've already learned, however, that Big Daddy, like many in the medical profession, will never admit to a patient that they've made a mistake. I assume it's the legal implications so I don't press the point. Rather, I make a bad joke: If the medieval Church possessed half the instruments I saw in radiology there wouldn't have been a single heretic in all of Europe! He laughs but it sounds forced.

Today, Big Daddy himself needs three sticks to get me going. I'm feeling miserable, angry, and sorry for myself, all at the same time. And, I'm disgusted with the whole sorry mess.

Oprah is on the TV above my chair (scheduling decreed that I temporarily do afternoons). But since the televisions in dialysis can only be heard through headphones, so as not to awaken those who wish to sleep, I cannot hear what she's saying. It must be something powerful, because the people around her seem to be crying. Yet without sound, it is difficult to say if Oprah is making them cry or they're weeping for some other reason.

An innocent, I've never watched Oprah or her ilk, the TV therapists and saviors, until the clinic. It's probably a good thing I can't hear her. Entertainment masking itself as enlightenment. It should be the other way around. Entertainment ought to mask a challenge. When someone asked him why he was begging from a statue, Diogenes the Cynic philosopher replied: "To get practice in being refused." You may laugh, but then you may also begin to think about how easy it is to turn to stone when confronted by the suffering of our fellow human beings. The very first sentence of philosopher Soren Kierkegaard's *Fear and Trembling*, written in 1843, describes the TV therapists perfectly: "Not merely in the realm of commerce but in the world of ideas as well our age is organizing a regular clearance sale."

Meanwhile, Oprah is smiling in perfect self-satisfaction, and blessing the faithful. The crowd is clapping and cheering (I'd guess . . . but maybe like me they've had enough?). It all seems designed to gratify but without challenging, without actual work, without danger.

An ancient Zen saying has it: "To become attached to one's own enlightenment is as much a sickness as attachment to one's ego. The profounder the enlightenment, the worse the illness."

Bart, the male nurse, escorts me out. This, too, is policy: The nurse who brings you from the waiting room takes you back out after treatment in case you suffer a post-dialysis collapse. As we walked out, Bart related this little tale: "You know, we had a patient here who came down with Alzheimer's. After that, she was never happier. It was simple things too, like fine weather, a gift of flowers, a piece of candy . . . all elicited cries of joy from the poor woman. This form of dementia cured her completely of her dialysis depression."

"Well, maybe I ought to suffer a stroke?"

Bart laughs. "I heard some expert on *Oprah* say that those who look on the bright side of things live longer while curmudgeons expire early."

"So don't be sad or angry. Accept?" Sarcasm fills my voice.

Bart, however, either ignores my bad humor, or has become accustomed to irritable kidney patients. "And last week I heard a UCLA psychologist conclude, after extensive study and testing, that those who try to face reality squarely have major mental problems, while those who put a positive spin—or what's called "positive imagery"—upon the experience of reality do not experience mental problems, anguish, or even anxiety."

I say slowly, "So, if the Buddha claimed to see into the reality of the world—his doctrine of *anicca*, impermanence—then he suffered mental problems?"

"According to the experts." Bart sounds uncertain.

"And also Heraclitus? Schopenhauer? Plato? Nietzsche? Even Jesus and the prophets?"

Bart looks puzzled. "Happy people live longer. Look on the bright side. Accept . . . the experts say."

I walk uncertainly to my car. Yes, I feel angry. Perhaps I am able to fully face this fact for the first time. I'm angry that this kidney failure happened to me, in mid-life—*me*, when so many others my age are perfectly healthy. Such anger is stupid and selfish. *Why not me?* I feel it nonetheless.

I'm angry at dumb genetics, angry with my father. It seems that I've had to live with this disease my entire life (I was seventeen when he was diagnosed). And I'm afraid, too—when I look at my own son and wonder if he's inherited a genetic time bomb from me.

And I say it aloud: "I do *not* accept!"

Then I recall what Dostoyevsky said about his epileptic fits. A few moments before the onset he experienced a feeling of happiness, of insight, of harmony, which is quite impossible to imagine in a "normal" state. And so he was driven to the paradoxical conclusion that the highest mode of existence, those gleams and flashes of the highest awareness, had to be considered the lowest. They were the result of a disease. And so what if it is? he concluded (*The Idiot*).

~

Some of hypertension is contextual, Dr. Jung once told me. It seems to be a disease of our fast-paced, tension-filled century. Would my kidneys have failed had my family remained in a small village on Sicily centuries ago? Fishing for honest fish, singing our hymns to the virgin, her son, the saints? All of us illiterate? Ha! I know better than to fall into a romantic reverie about history. Would I have lived to my present age, even without kidney failure? Death might have come from cold steel, lead poisoning, or, more probably, the heretic's fiery ascension. Or, death might have come swiftly had I been caught gazing too long upon the lovely person of some earth nymph.

That morning, arriving home, I find a letter informing me that I'm officially on the kidney transplant list. The wait for a person of my blood type, says the bold type, is eighteen months.

Jesusmaryjosephandallthesaints . . .

## ❧ 9 ❧

# Dolorous Abyss

(Dante, Inferno, Canto 4)

Today, a Monday, spasms in my arm prevented proper blood flow. The problem persisted through the entire three and a half hours. Momma Cass inserted the needles; she *always* gets them in without trouble and with perfect blood flow. But not today. More evidence for indeterminacy. I talk to her.

She tells me that she "loves" dialysis nursing.

Did she lose a parent or a loved one to kidney disease?

"No. I just love it here. We can really help people."

Yet the poor pay, the long hours, the dangers of handling blood—the depressed nature of the place?

"I love my work."

I wonder if this is sincere or another aspect of therapy. The nurses must have been instructed in the arts of patient interaction. The kidneys may not be the only artificial organs in this clinic.

Yet, Momma Cass sounds sincere. Why doubt her? Rather, compared to so many others in this society, she is a saint. She really has helped.

She turns away and occupies herself opening plastic bags of tubing, bags of saline, preparing needles and gauze for the next shift of midday patients, which begins at about 11:30 a.m. There's a third shift, mostly working people who arrive around 4 p.m. and stay till 8:30 p.m. All three shifts number from twenty to thirty patients.

Meanwhile, the buddhas are arguing about the merits of the morning talk shows. The threats fly; voices are raised. The show under consideration is called *The View*: three women sitting around a table, drinking coffee (I'd guess), talking. The nurses and female patients love it; the male nurses and patients would rather watch sixties and seventies reruns on cable. Glancing at the screen, I see that a fourth woman has joined the group. She's obviously famous, but I don't recognize her, and without sound, do not know her name. However, the discussion in clinic is far more animated than on the screen. Real life always beats third-rate stage plays. In the end the nurses win and the show remains on. The nurses always win.

Angry and frustrated, the buddhas turn to discussing problems with Medicare. On this shift, I'm the only one who still maintains a job and whose insurance pays the costs of treatment.

Jake, next to me, worked for the railroad, and he says that he'd still like to work even now, and probably could be useful on his off days from the clinic. But given the business obsession with hours and pay, this is impossible. He tells stories about the small towns along the railroad line years ago. An African-American dare not step off the train in many of these places. To me these towns sound like foreign countries I've visited, say those of Eastern Europe.

The citizenry of some towns, he goes on, are heavily armed; local government is a paper fiction for the outside world. Still, he enjoyed working and regrets the enforced retirement. This would be the best therapy for anyone with chronic illness.

Jake's stories run out and he sleeps. The nurses are talking among themselves, mostly about work schedules, days off, weekends. Since one shift goes Tuesdays, Thursdays and Saturdays, everyone must work a Saturday. Hence, there always seems to be bargaining going on among the nurses, swapping days, making deals, which seems far more important than patients.

I'm left alone. Today, in Gibbon's second volume, it's the Vandals in North Africa. The Vandals were Arian heretics, believing that Jesus, although divine, was a lesser creature than God the Father (there was a time, said the African priest Arius, when the Son *was not*). The towns of the North African coast were Nicene, holding that Jesus was of the same essence as the Father—*homoosious* in the Greek of the creed (I wonder what the historical Yeshua, a Jew, would have thought about all this Greek gibberish). The outraged Vandals burned, tortured, raped, and murdered their Christian brothers and sisters over this issue. Gibbon goes into gleeful lengths describing the bloodshed.

So much suffering—natural, man-made. Glancing at the nurses, I experience an overwhelming yet inexpressible feeling of appreciation, respect, admiration. Anyone who serves to relieve the smallest bit of human suffering deserves society's greatest praise, and material support. Like Momma Cass, they're all saints. And finally, I see wings.

Sometimes I'll tell the nurses and doctors stories of my running exploits. I'm sure they don't believe a word. They cannot imagine how anyone in my condition could have run marathons in two hours and thirty minutes. I'm exaggerating, like many other patients.

Then I remember the ancient Greek story of Diagoras of Rhodes. Diagoras won the boxing at the 79th Olympiad, in 464 B.C.E. He was much admired, called *euthymaches*, fair fighter. At the 83rd Olympiad two of his sons won Olympic crowns. Diagoras was in the stadium for his sons' victories. The crowd surrounded him, congratulating and embracing him in joy. His sons ran to him, placed the crowns on the old man's head, and then hoisted him onto their shoulders, carrying him in a victory lap around the stadium to the cheers of all Hellas.

Suddenly, amid the ovations, a Spartan voice called out from the crowd: "Die now, Diagoras! Nothing remains but to ascend Olympus." The Spartan voice, we are told, did not carry envy or malice, but was inspired by fear of the gods lest this great joy slip into impiety, the sin of hubris or thinking oneself like a god.

Diagoras heard the voice, knew what it meant. On the shoulders of his sons, before all Greece, he bowed his head and breathed his last.

"Die now . . . "

I look at the machine, the artificial kidney, the tubing, the nurses bustling about, and I remember those days when I ran in the marathons, healthy and full of energy, happy.

"Die now."

Is this hubris, this clinging to life at any cost?

Suddenly, one of the older patients experiences a machine breakdown. The damned thing abruptly springs a leak! Before anyone can get to him, there is a pool of blood on the floor, growing by the second, and the poor old man faints away. The nurses fly to the machine. I've never seen them move so fast. Quickly they disconnect him, shut down the machine, and wheel in another. They hook him up to the new machine, pump in the saline, and he revives. Others are mopping up the floor. In a few minutes it is over and everything is back to normal. The event leaves me shaken, for this can easily happen to me. Diagoras of Rhodes . . . die now, Tony!

That same session an old lady goes into arrest. The fire department rescue arrives and carries her out on a stretcher, bound for the emergency room. A stroke probably. I never see her again.

Life no longer burns with a great flame, in me or any of the other patients; life is more like a flickering candle, dull points of fragile illumination in the clinic gloom. The slightest breeze blows it out. Again, we are the marginal people. Yet, this afternoon, I will still go out for a run, asserting life, feeding a little the fire. The outward absurdity of the act makes me laugh loudly. Vicki passes by and shakes her head. It's the toxins.

∼

Christmas is coming. The nurses decorate the clinic, but it's all snowmen, elves, Santas, winter scenes; nothing about Jesus, Yeshua in my bad Hebrew, which surprises me.

Today I get to Gibbon's account of St. Augustine, "He boldly sounded the dark abyss of grace, predestination, free will, and original sin," Gibbon writes. And he goes on to say that it was Augustine who framed the "rigid system" of Christianity.

"Dark abyss." The words resonate but I can't say exactly why. Perhaps it's this half-life? Perhaps the constant reminder of death? I think of a bad joke: My wounds could be a modern version of the stigmata. Yet I've been pierced many more times than poor Yeshua.

Nietzsche said something like bad jokes are better than no jokes. I often quote this to my students, and they usually groan. But I dare not tell such jokes in the clinic.

Apparently God doesn't laugh. No. God does laugh! The patients are glued to one of those infernal morning talk shows. I put on the headphones.

Today the subject is the beating death of a gay student from the University of Wyoming. He was tied to a fence and left to die. Following this news story is the clip of a Christian minister from Topeka who travels about the country attacking gays. He and his followers parade with signs that read: "When a fag dies, God laughs." Another sign reads: "AIDS, God's cure for fags." In disgust I tear off the headphones so as not to hear what the holy minister is saying. Hopefully, he is interpreting the passages, which cannot be Christian, given how Yeshua ministered love and healing to the sick and the "lost sheep" of Israel.

In historical context, symbolically, the cure of the sick—illness being ritual pollution and thus condemned by the Torah—demonstrates the savior's inclusiveness, and his *radicalism*. Or, many would like to think so. As usual, I'm doubtful. Leviticus condemns homosexuality more as a corruption, a pollution, an abomination, moral impurity as opposed to ritual impurity; the Hebrew word is *to'evah*. Yeshua may be building a fence around the Torah like any good Jewish rabbi.

In later tales of the rabbis, God sends Moses down to sit in class, and sometimes even God needs to learn a thing or two about the law (torah, with a lowercase "t" also means instruction).

The patients, good Christians all, seem to be enjoying the "news." They, like God, also hate fags. The worst epitaph one buddha can throw at another is "gay." Terrible threats generally follow such an insult. I find this sad and amusing at the same time. I can only guess at what the historical Yeshua might say.

My friend Yakob told me this story: Some years ago at our university, a gay student named Ed ran for Homecoming Queen. This occurred at the time when gays were beginning to "come out." Ed ran a brilliant campaign. So the sororities trotted out the least likely candidates, not wishing to be the first to lose a serious homecoming race to a real drag queen.

And Ed was quite the looker in drag. His campaign went something like: "Don't vote for a wannabe. Vote for a real Queen—Ed."

Ed could have won. But the state governor refused to accept the election, and by backdoor manipulation a true femme was named queen. In those days the governor came down from the state Capitol and kissed the queen at mid-field during half time. Ed couldn't wait for this moment in history. He spent days preparing—his best dress, his makeup, what he'd say. . . .

Alas, it never happened. The governor, like God, hated fags.

Poor Ed.

∽

This Friday after treatment, I go to the eye clinic. I walk in with another nauseating headache; they took off a record amount of fluid in order to lower my blood pressure. My pressure fluctuated erratically throughout the dialysis session, but at the end it was still high, one hundred and fifty over a hundred.

The eye clinic is crowded; the average wait is an hour. Finally I'm ushered into the examining room. I explain my situation. The doctor begins the tests. My headache gets worse. He squirts chemicals into my eyes to dilate them. I try not to flinch or complain, but the chemicals sting and do wonders for my headache. He shines a sharp, pinpoint of light into my eyes. I imagine (and not for the last time) how some of the prisoners must have felt when given various forms of "treatment" in Stalin's gulags.

At last, it is over. The verdict: I need stronger glasses for reading. The fluid shifts will cause vision changes; I'll have to learn to live with them.

Staggering out of the hospital, I spend nearly half an hour searching for my car. The daylight—a sunny, cloudless late autumn afternoon—assaults my eyes. Everything dissolves into frightful glare. Somehow, nearly blind, I negotiate the drive home. A short run that evening cures my headache.

Walking through the museums of the Vatican, my children, then ages five and ten, were fascinated by the many paintings of St. Sebastian. The poor saint was martyred, tied to a stake and perforated by numerous arrows. We spent hours examining the various representations of the holy sufferer, executed in a thousand different scenes by the same method. St. Sebastian, patron saint of dialysis!

~

Am I developing a "kidney personality?" I've heard the term whispered about the clinic, in the hospital; Dr. Jung has upon occasion made oblique references to it.

A kidney personality finds it difficult to be sociable, bordering on the misanthropic (have my kidneys been failing for my whole life?). A kidney personality is moody, depressed (again that word!), but also angry, irritable, prone to fly into sudden rages or drop like lead into depths of morose lethargy. Walking misery, a KP is the strongest social repellent.

My three children demand a certain level of social interaction. Through them I come into contact with parents, teachers, and other people at sports events, school gatherings, birthday parties. Is it KP that forces me into isolation, withdrawal, avoidance? I seem to hear nothing but banalities, anxious materialism—childish minds trying to seem important.

Perhaps it's a simple lack of energy. I can no longer repress feelings that were always there. I don't have the strength to maintain the public persona, the mask we all wear. It could be as simple as this: When you feel lousy, you don't want to talk to people.

In *The Psychopathology of Everyday Life*, Freud talks about forgetting: One wants to forget something but doesn't want to forget, or one forgets and yet doesn't forget at the same time.

This appears to resemble my dilemma. I want to participate in family activities—I'm fairly certain of this—but I don't want to take part. At the same time! I don't want people around oozing sympathy, yet I feel isolated and alone, a pariah. Those things that interest most people seem utterly banal, shallow, and hardly worth the effort.

By December, nearly four months on dialysis, my kidney personality has taken over. Yet, at times I wonder: Maybe illness has forced me to see things more clearly. I lack the energy to fool myself. Depression could be seeing the world as it truly is and no longer telling ourselves soothing fables. Maybe wrong blood pressure has led to "right view." I need to surrender depressing beliefs, the psychologists might say. Yet, they cannot say that these do not represent reality.

And I recall a passage from the Buddhist sutras: "But, oh Bhikkus, rare in this world are those who enjoy freedom from mental illness even for a moment, except those who are free from mental defilements."

# Part III

# Daffy

# ⇐ 10 ⇒

# Lust and Law

(DANTE, INFERNO, CANTO 5)

Today, Wednesday, December 2, a clinic administrator brings an older African-American gentleman
into the dialysis unit to meet me. He is Chairman of the
Black Studies Department at our state university, and he's
suffering my illness, hypertension, but is not quite ready
for dialysis.

During our conversation, I discover—from the
administrator—many of my fellow patients are illiterate!
This comes as something of a surprise. I can hardly imagine a world without books, and it strikes me suddenly how
narrow such a world must be. Instantly their TV addiction becomes comprehensible.

The Chairman thinks it amusing that I'm reading
Gibbon. I come close to asking what he would read, but
swallow the question and ask instead about his family,
whether his family, like mine, bears a history of hypertension. It did—his mother.

I try to sound upbeat, undoubtedly what the administrator desired.

"Oh yes, you'll feel better on dialysis." (Not exactly
true. Some days it's so; some days you feel just as bad as
before treatments.)

"It's fairly painless." (Not exactly true either, especially when they miss the fistula, or the fistula spasms, or you get Nurse Peggy.)

"You'll feel like . . . uh . . . you've done a shift of yard work after treatments." (True, if your yard is an eighteen-hole golf course.)

The administrator drags him off, her purpose accomplished.

Such a dichotomy: They're keeping me alive, and I do feel better, but I resent it, hate it, feel trapped. My bad jokes, quiet blasphemy, obnoxious comments are all a protest. Paul Celan once said: "I hope to be able to blaspheme to the end."

Returning to Gibbon, the very next passage reads: "When it comes to theological disputes," he's talking about the schism between the Orthodox and the Catholics, "an atom becomes a monster."

~

Now that radiology has pronounced on my arm, the clinic is out of excuses.

My fistula is simply lousy, they say. It spasms. It's hard to stick because it curves and actually moves at the touch.

In fact, the frequency of such events appears to be rising, along with my blood pressure. The machine is constantly buzzing, the red lights flashing as if they're part of the new Christmas decorations flooding the unit. The sticking problem is getting worse: Two sticks a session has become a rare occurrence, like a gift from the gods.

It's December, the days short, dark, and depressing; and it's winter—the season of death.

But it's also Christmas, the coming birthday of our Lord.

One day, I break my vow of silence and teach the nurses a little history, and take a perverse joy in the telling:

I explain the winter solstice to them. "In the northern hemisphere, the sun traverses the sky with the least elevation off the horizon, hence the shortest day. In the ancient world, this meant the death of the sun. And the sun was a god: Sol Invictus, Mithra, Amon-Re, Apollo, so on.

"For days the sun remains dead, at least to the naked eye. The sun god is gone. But then—oh, great joy—on December 25th, the sun appears a little higher off the horizon and the day is a little longer. The sun has begun its long climb to the spring equinox and ultimately the summer solstice. The sun is reborn—*it's the sun's birthday!* And before Constantine became Emperor with the help of the Christians, his personal god was the sun god. Why confuse the masses? When was Christ born? Constantine knew: December 25th. Do you understand the concept of syncretism in religion? Oh yes, our god is really your god, with a new name.

"No one knows when Yeshua was really born. You have a 364 to 1 chance it is Christmas. And we historians can't nail down the year either. The birth narratives in Matthew and Luke contradict one another, and between the two Gospels, poor Yeshua's birth is a full *ten years apart*—they can't even agree on his grandfather!"

Now I'm known in the clinic as the grinch who stole Christmas.

"Oh, no need for concern," I laugh. "No one cares what foolish professors of history say. Ever since Christmas was swallowed up by capitalism, no amount of historical analysis, no matter how well documented—no sun's birthday—will ever challenge the holiday. Jesus was born on December 25th as long as capitalism says so. Not God or Constantine, but economics is omnipotent."

None of this does me any good. And I seem to have forgotten that some of these believers may get the chance to crucify me with their needles.

～

Suddenly one of the older patients goes into convulsions. He's two chairs from me, the one they call Captain because of the tattoos covering his body. Before they can get a pan beneath his chin, he vomits like a fountain, spewing all over himself, the floor, even the machine. His eyes roll back and he passes out.

The nurses are frantic. Vicki shuts off the machine. Madonna opens the valve on the saline and squeezes the plastic bag. Even Big Daddy rushes over to help.

The corpsman goes to the desk and makes a phone call. In a short time, three paramedics arrive wheeling in a stretcher. They appear to be familiar with the clinic, coming in the back door, dodging the machines, acting with determination.

Captain is still lifeless. They pull his needles. The paramedics lift him out of the chair—his arms dangle and his head lolls—and they strap him down to the stretcher. They clear his mouth and throat and cover his face with a plastic breathing mask that is connected by a tube to an oxygen tank. Then they wheel him out. The entire operation takes less than fifteen minutes.

I never see Captain again. Afraid to ask, I never hear if he's alive or if he died in the hospital.

Today, December 17, I glance up from Gibbon and see from the silent TV screens that American bombs are falling upon Mesopotamia. We're going after Saddam again. America's helots, I think silently; most of the buddhas are cheering.

I'm sad, feeling empathy for the suffering my country is causing in the cradle of Western civilization. No matter what their politics, their beliefs, circumstances, reasons, all those who suffer touch me deeply. Depression breeds empathy for Iraq. How terrible.

I'm not even interested, however, in Clinton's continuing problems. The Monica affair began about the same time Dr. Jung called with the bad news that my creatinine was near ten and I should be on dialysis immediately. The day I started down my own ninefold path, "Billy Blow Job," as the buddhas call him, started on his path leading to impeachment.

But for me now, my blood flowing into this machine, Billy's problems are elevator music. I feel infinitely more for Iraq.

I first came to the clinic after August 17, the date of Billy's public confession. The patients, naturally, had long arrived at their own consensus: "Everybody knows that Arkansas boy fucked around."

During September, the buddhas were still interested in the unfolding scandal. Every morning, the screens were crowded with the likes of Starr, Monica, Congress, Bill, and Hillary. The comedy unfolded as I became acquainted with dialysis—one cannot call it a tragedy. Shakespeare would have certainly written it as a comedy, perhaps a Bill soliloquy with him crying "O, what a rogue and peasant slave am I!"

By December, however, the patients are fed up with Billy Blow Job. Jake tells me why: "Rompin' in the White House ain't no big deal. Don't like his choice of women, though. Monica's pretty greasy. But he didn't do it like a man. That's wrong!"

Jake and the others agree. The President of the United States ought to be a role model. Billy's antics are un-American. If he wanted to be like JFK, well then, according to the buddhas, he should have done it proper, real intercourse, "like a man."

That's what they said. The wisdom of the dialysis clinic.

December 18 begins the House hearings on Clinton's impeachment. I watch some. Curious, I even put on the headphones to listen to the debates. After a few minutes, I go back to Gibbon. It appears that acting has replaced intelligence and character as the prerequisite for public office. Everyone seems to be playing to the audience.

In Gibbon, I'm with the Moslems at the gates of Granada, a drama far more profound and exciting than what unfolds on the TV.

Still, I glance up from time to time. Ultimately curiosity fades and I stick with Gibbon. Surely classic TV was better theater than these hearings.

There's a story about Alec Guinness: A young boy and his mother accosted the actor. The mom told him that her son had seen the Star Wars trilogy eight times! Sir Alec wagged a finger at the youth and said: "Don't you ever watch another minute of that disgusting twaddle!" The kid ran away crying; his mom was horrified. People just can't distinguish anymore the actor from the man. Actors act.

And I read this: Discussing the Byzantines, Gibbon says,

> The rage of war, inherent to the human species, could not be healed by evangelic precepts of charity and peace; and the ambition of the Catholic princes has renewed in every age the calamities of hostile contention.

This for Starr.

About Peter the Hermit (the first crusade), Gibbon writes:

> Peter supplied the deficiency of reason by loud and frequent appeals to Christ and his mother, to the saints and angels of paradise, with whom he had personally conversed.

This for the Judiciary Committee.

About Pope Urban II preaching crusade at Claremont, Gibbon says:

> His topics were obvious, his exhortation was vehement, his success was inevitable.

Pick one.

∾

I've been able to doze a little on the machine. Sleeping soundly is not an option. I'm still far too frightened that something might go wrong. And the nurses take blood pressure every half hour. But being able to doze is a victory. *L'Affaire* Bill is good for insomnia.

The dialysis clinic routine never changes, except for one day, Sol Invictus day. No treatments for the supposed birthday of the Hebrew named Yeshua. I'm to come into the clinic on Saturday.

On this day, the day after Christmas, I'm able to doze through most of the treatment. And as I hover in that borderland region between consciousness and dreams, my mind drifts back in time and treads again upon the twisting path that brought me here.

The question, it appears, exists in both realms, dreams and consciousness: How did I ever get into this mess?

# ⧼ 11 ⧽

# O Credulous Mankind

(DANTE, INFERNO, CANTO 7)

*Make good medicine from the suffering of sickness.*
—Kyong Ho, Zen Master

June, 1994: I've just completed another one of those miserable four hour Glomerular Filtration Rate (GFR) tests. Again, samples of urine and blood measure the radioactive material processed by my kidneys, hence how effectively those microscopic glomeruli, the working apparatus of the nephron, are transferring waste products into the urine. The results, communicated that afternoon by Dr. Jung, indicate that my kidney function is declining. The number he gives me measures the ability of the kidney to process toxins in the blood in a given time. In 1992, my number stood at thirty-two. Normal would be in the nineties, even one hundred. A year later, it was thirty, still margin enough for error. Today it stands at twenty-six. There can no longer be any doubt. The decline is linear.

Dr. Jung, calculator in hand, says that in four years I'll be on dialysis. It turned out to be a pretty accurate prophecy.

I come home from the hospital quite shaken. This is unacceptable. I'm not my father! Rage, anger, frustration . . . fear!

But after a few days, my spirits improve. After all, there are still no symptoms: No fatigue . . . oh yes there's fatigue, yet that's due to the blood pressure medicines. There can be no doubting the numbers, it is true, but numbers mean nothing without interpretation. The history and philosophy of science teach that measurement does not always reflect reality. Measurement has the tendency to reification.

Furthermore, Dr. Jung's calculations appear to be a fine illustration of determinism. The medical profession makes its pronouncement: You are sick. And behold, the illness progresses just as predicted. But is it mechanistic processes in the cells? Or, is it acceptance of the decree?

Dr. Jung told me numerous times that medicine does not know why the kidneys spiral down into complete failure even after the assumed cause, high blood pressure, has been removed. This puzzle, however, is due to the present state of knowledge. Someday medicine will understand the mechanisms. Nonetheless, its predictions are still accurate. The calculations are deterministic. And, so too, my kidneys.

But modern physics, I reasoned, especially after the late twenties, has questioned absolute determinism. Quantum theory (the mechanics of the atom) says that there's an inherent indeterminism in nature. Heisenberg's uncertainty principle demonstrates that one cannot simultaneously measure momentum and position of a subatomic particle. Predictability can hope only for an accuracy governed by statistical probability.

Sitting in my dialysis chair, in this semiconscious state the day after Christmas in 1998, four years later, feeling the dull pain of the needles in my arm, the inevitability of renal failure now seems as though it was written in concrete.

Not then. I had so many good reasons to question the prediction. Good philosophy. Perfect logic. Perfectly rational objections.

~

We can find the best and most foolproof reasons for ignoring what we really know. What feels good must be true. Gullibility can formulate the best arguments, and I became Professor "Daffy."

I discovered all sorts of reasons to ignore the numbers.

I canceled visits with Dr. Jung, always finding some good reason: Classes were too demanding; another engagement took priority; I was working on a book that I could not abandon without losing the thread.

All good reasons. All perfectly rational.

Then in August of 1994, on a Saturday, I discovered yet another reason to reject medical prophecy. At a local bookstore, I spied a title: *Quantum Healing*. The author was an endocrinologist named Deepak Chopra. I'd never heard of this Chopra, although I'd studied most of the popular and scholarly literature on quantum theory. But the book had little to do with quantum theory.

Chopra talked a great deal about Ayurvedic medicine, the healing techniques of ancient India. I was familiar with the Vedanta philosophy (Indian philosophy based on the Upanishads) and I knew the differences within the many yoga traditions. Zazen had been my practice since my military service, but I'd never considered it as physical healing, which only strengthened the ego-self and denied the reality of impermanence. Now came the real final exam in Buddhism. Thus came Chopra.

Chopra's apocryphal tales of spontaneous healing raised my hopes. His testimony was mesmerizing. Looking back, however, "apocryphal tales" better fit his little stories, since any chronic physical illness is a maddeningly complex condition, and improvement at any point in time may be a mirage.

Yet, in 1995 I was bedazzled. Optimism broke through the dark clouds of illness like some blinding light on the Damascus road. If western science had pronounced me doomed, there was Chopra.

It is astounding how the critical faculties may suddenly shut off like a switch. It is like a reprieve from an execution; as Dostoevsky describes in his diary and again in *The Idiot*, the victim is overwhelmed and intoxicated: One becomes a believer. When the ego-self is most in danger is when it becomes irresistible.

Dr. Jung once explained that everyone's blood pressure rose and fell during the day. Taking a single reading is like a snapshot. So he made me wear a bulky monitor for an entire day. Computerized and battery operated, it inflated every half hour and registered my pressure. I taught my classes that day without the students ever catching on. The results of this 1994 experiment said that the medications had my blood pressure controlled. In fact, Dr. Jung worried that it was too low.

Blood pressure, only in those who are susceptible, can rise with stress. Even after the objective cause of the stress has been removed, the effects of the stress in elevated blood pressure linger on like a molecular or cellular memory.

Chopra called the idea of cellular memory a "valuable clue." Blood pressure is controlled by the autonomic nervous system; but no, says Chopra, it may be mastered by meditation and visualization techniques of Ayurvedic medicine. Blood pressure, among other things, may be brought under conscious control.

But where does quantum theory enter the picture? Save for a few offhand remarks and bland approbation concerning the founders—Einstein, Bohr, Heisenberg, Pauli,

Schrodinger, etc.—Chopra never said exactly, except for what seemed to me vague references to consciousness and wave collapse—a highly contentious subject among the physicists I knew. Somehow, according to Master Deepak, quantum theory supported Ayurvedic medicine and the practices of the Maharishi Mahesh Yogi.

Such blank places did not deter me. I read the book, pulled old sutras off the shelves, and started to practice. Every morning at 5:30, I would meditate for forty-five minutes, not to control blood pressure but *to heal*. Focusing on my kidneys—I even had Dr. Jung point out their location by tapping my back—I attempted to visualize healing. I *saw* the nephrons growing red and healthy, processing the toxins. The sutras advised the patient to change attitude, to become bright, cheerful, happy. No more resentment, no more worry, anxiety, frustration (like our California psychologist). And so I did.

∽

It is the first Monday of the new year, 1999, and I experience a blood spurting episode. Now it can no longer be said that I am a dialysis neophyte.

My nurse for the day, the one they call Grandma, constantly wanders about the clinic as if she's lost. She cannot see my machine's red lights, nor does she hear the more subdued time's-up buzzer. Deep in conversation with another nurse, she is annoyed when it becomes apparent her presence is required at my machine.

It takes an eternity for Grandma to cross the great spaces between chairs.

She shuts down the machine and gives me saline, cleaning the kidney and tubes of my blood. She rips the plastic tape off my arm; the next step is to remove the needles.

Preoccupied, still talking, she pulls the first needle, but too slowly . . . SPLASH! Blood shoots like a pressurized fountain, nearly three yards! She begins stuffing gauze bandages over the wounds, which instantly become red and soggy.

More gauze . . . She squeezes my arm hard. The pain is hardly equal to the stress. Finally the blood flow is stopped. My clothes are soaked. I must look shaken, for she says: "Don't worry, you ain't lost much. These things happen."

She wanders off to resume her interrupted conversation, leaving me to hold the wounds for about fifteen minutes—to make sure.

In search of distraction, I glance up at the TV screen. Oprah is interviewing Gary Zukav. I read Zukav's book, *The Dancing Wu Li Masters*, about quantum theory and mysticism. I'd read many such books, but the historian in me always rebelled against the ahistorical juxtaposition of modern physicists and ancient gurus. I knew the great difficulty of trying to grasp the world of antiquity, east or west. I knew the problem of the sources, that none are without corruption. Likewise, I'd struggled with the mathematics of quantum theory, the difficulty of translating the abstract functions into physical events.

"What's he saying?" I ask Jake, who's watching.

"Somethin' 'bout self-realization. Hey, man, how's your arm?"

"I think the bleeding's stopped."

"Shit like that happens," Jake observes.

"Does Oprah agree with him?" I ask. But the question isn't necessary. Oprah is nodding and smiling her approval. She's telling us to listen to Gary. We all need to listen. Another new savior. A latent messianic.

As Oprah blesses the audience with a rehearsed beatific smile, and Zukav looks on with self-satisfaction, I think back to Deepak.

# ⁓ 12 ⁓

# Ice

(Dante, Inferno, Canto 34)

Late fall of 1995: I was suffering from the cold, even though the freezing temperatures had yet to arrive. It was a deep chill, one no amount of clothing could insulate; the cold seemed to touch the very core of my being.

One may suffer kidney failure for a long time and still not experience symptoms. They come on so slowly, and the body adapts so deviously, a person hardly notices the small retreats and surrenders, the inches conceded. In this way, the disease is particularly vicious and deceiving. I felt cold, yet I'd been cold before.

Without debilitating symptoms, the patient's natural inclination is to doubt the physician's warnings. In fact, the physician becomes the enemy: I feel fine, but he says I'm sick and will end up on dialysis. Damn liar!

The most compassionate and well-meaning physician in the world—and Dr. Jung exemplified these qualities—became a devil. Just the sight of him was a reminder, a warning, and a threat. He was a walking accusation that shouts: DENIAL! When he asked me how I was feeling, there were barbed hooks in the question—he *knew* and I didn't want to know.

I avoided Dr. Jung. There were all sorts of good reasons to miss appointments, as I've said, and I discovered new ones.

Meanwhile, I pressed on through Deepak, practicing daily meditation. I studied the Upanishads, the yoga sutras, raja meditation, kundalini chakra yoga, Tibetan yoga, including *The Book of the Dead*. I told myself that I felt better. I *did* feel better.

But the chill persisted, deepened. It proved very easy to forget Nietzsche's aphorism: Proof by potency—it feels good therefore it must be true.

During the last week of December, 1995, I went out for a late-afternoon run; the temperature was fairly mild for that season, mid-thirties, and the sun was bright. The run was my only physical activity for that day. My legs felt particularly heavy, despite moving in slow motion. A lethargic blanket had settled over me. Perhaps it was simply a bad day; the blood pressure medicines have a tendency to cause fatigue.

There were many good reasons for being cold and tired, other than the symptoms of kidney failure.

$\sim$

Around the age forty-two, I noticed a sharp rise in all my race times; I'd run my last marathon ten years before, and these races were mainly five and ten kilometers. It seemed the old "kick," a surge of speed I once called up at will, had evaporated, just drained away like some leaky water pipe. Naturally, I was busy with other, more important activities: teaching, writing, parenting. I was getting older. Naturally.

In age group races I lost regularly, losing to individuals I could beat easily a few years ago. I needed to adjust my training, I told myself. Perhaps the lethargy came from over-training.

In March of 1995, telling myself that I did indeed feel better, I entered a local five kilometer road race. Here was a truly "objective" measurement. Meditating for six months, trying to put Deepak into practice, I used the race to measure my progress.

The race told me what I already knew but had not the courage to acknowledge. Even the tiny dust-mop dogs beat me. My pride was stung and my self-image in ruins, which is real healing according to the Buddha and which I had conveniently forgotten—mindfulness can be summarized in one phrase: Remember to remember.

I swore never to race again. Actually, this wasn't a conscious decision at all, not a verbal decision.

I hadn't been practicing alternative medicine long enough, I told myself. That was the reason for the poor showing. Patience . . . more time in practice is what I needed. My kidneys were healing. I felt better.

The kidney produces a hormone called erythropoietin (EPO) that tells the bone marrow to manufacture red blood cells. Red blood cells carry oxygen to the muscles from the lungs. More efficient breathing—the breathing exercises of meditation—means extra oxygen, but it does no good without the carrier molecule.

With kidney failure, these EPO producing cells die and the hematocrit, a measure of the percentage of red blood cells in the blood, falls. Below thirty-five, one begins to suffer anemia; below thirty, a deep body cold and constant fatigue. As they say in the clinic: "There's no gas in the tank." I think of it as a dead battery: The engine would barely start, finally not at all.

∾

And so, my running went into a precipitous decline. This decline was measurable, but only if I raced. No races, no measurement, no decline. There were many reasons, all quite good, not to race. Yet I still ran—had to take Misha out, poor dog.

However, a more subtle, insidious decline occurred, far beneath the surface of awareness.

Life—the daily activities of simply living, the amusements, labor, social interactions, chit-chat, tasks, chores and habits—began to lose its hold and I began to lose interest. Words can merely point to the experience—even now I marvel at how quiet and sneaky the steady decline, like the drip, drip of water wearing away a chunk of granite. First, it became an imposition to do things, then a chore, finally a struggle. Going out to dinner, to a movie, to one of my children's sports events, to an open house at their school, even playing board games with the kids—a thousand small, insignificant things that one hardly thinks about, became a major test of will and self-discipline. Merely *thinking* about doing something made me tired. And here was Deepak telling me to be happy when I hardly possessed the energy to smile.

The descent happened in tiny increments, over the course of years, like the creeping advance of a glacier. The gradual decline, much as Gibbon describes happening to Rome, remained invisible to me, or, to put it another way, I turned my head and looked away. Another age might have called it melancholy, although it seemed to me far darker than that. But an outside observer, watching carefully, could mark the gradual winding-down, indeed of the very desire to live.

My poor wife Armine was that observer. A nurse herself (rehabilitating heart patients), she recognized the signs. What ensued was a kind of struggle between us; she strained to make me see and I refused to look.

I could still run. It became easy to gauge everything else by that single fact. Actions express the inner life. If I could still run, well then, I wasn't really ill inside.

But, oh, how slow those runs! What a daily effort of will power! I proved the bootstrap theory of subatomic physics: I pulled myself out of my chair every day. I fought a battle every day, only to be overwhelmed by colossal odds.

Sometimes watching TV, or a movie, I'd casually wonder how people had the energy to even act. How absurd to think such a thing! Yet, the thought floated up, perhaps from that constant cold place inside.

An unanticipated insight arose with this creeping entropy of the spirit: I glimpsed, as never before, the utter transparency of advertisement, its attempt to create a value system in which the product, whatever that may be, becomes the royal road to happiness. Ironically, slow death brought in its wake a certain freedom from desire. And attempts to stimulate desire now appeared pointless and laughable. Already a kind of corpse, looking on from the outside and no longer bound by ties of energy, capitalist culture took on the look of a massive drug addiction, the media being the pushers.

Funny how freedom came with illness, immunity with kidney failure. The obvious manipulation only caused me to laugh. But it also made me sad; he whom the gods would destroy they first drive mad.

Yet, illness also brought a kind of gullibility. Perhaps the bone-deep realization of one's mortality, actually *feeling* the decline, destroys one's critical faculties. Subsequently a person grasps for any miserable piece of wreckage that floats past, as long as that wreckage has attached to it a note that bears a promise.

For me Deepak was that false promise. What, after all, did quantum theory have to do with Eastern alternative medicine? Nearly twenty years ago, in a book titled *Quantum Questions*, Ken Wilber had warned that mixing with modern physics would be the last thing in the world a true eastern mystic would desire. Memory, especially sober and critical memory, is apparently subject to the tyranny of toxins—I'd forgotten Wilber's warning.

Every morning, in good weather or foul, I seated myself on the deck and practiced one of the esoteric traditions. My aging runner's legs did not fold properly, and the best that I could do was an aching, laughable cross-legged perch.

I counted breaths, regulating breathing. Concentrating on the going-in and the breathing-out, I visualized the prana breath circulating through my body, energizing my shrinking kidneys. I felt them growing healthy, fresh, and revitalized.

I chanted Tibetan mantras, studied the chakra system, and tried to unleash the energy of kundalini, driving it into my kidneys.

All of this was terribly difficult, and I was practicing without the aid of a guru. But I had the original sources, the yoga sutras. In them, however, I began to sense a completely alien world, constructed by utterly strange individuals, from a world in time that no longer existed. This warning, too, I ignored.

One cannot drastically alter the inner without a major change in the outer. Healing required a complete and total transformation of life. The ties of family and profession were too strong, too complex, like the knot of

Gordian. Unlike Alexander, I lacked the strength to cut the knot and conquer Asia.

I needed a guru. . . . Only later would I grasp the wisdom of an old Tibetan precept: "One must know that disease is also a guru."

And so, I studied the sources as if possessed, trying to pick up Sanskrit again after many years of neglect. My toxin-loaded beaner couldn't hold the sacred language— at the same time, I was vainly struggling to continue my work on ancient Greek and Hebrew. The different scripts became jumbled. Chaos resulted. Confusion.

And all the time my kidneys slowly failed.

## ⁓ 13 ⁓

# Practicing Alchemy

(DANTE, INFERNO, CANTO 29)

Madonna (the singer, not the nurse) is on TV. Jake, wearing headphones, tells me that Madonna is talking about yoga and her spiritual teacher, the marvelous Deepak Chopra.

"What?" I gasp in mock astonishment, "Madonna's spiritual urges? Television always keeps us abreast of the irrelevant."

Oprah and Madonna irrelevant? Jake shakes his head in disbelief. Naturally, I'm joking (this from someone who sits reading Gibbon!).

I glance up at the screen. Madonna is gesturing; no, she's singing. Without sound it looks like comedy.

And sitting there in the dialysis chair, it strikes me: Deepak Chopra is Madonna's guru.

Quantum Healing . . . what does quantum have to do with healing?

The idea that somehow consciousness influences matter on the subatomic level because of the so-called collapse—of the Schrodinger wave function, which before it is observed is an array of probabilities—I think this is what he means.

Deepak wrote about that?

Not quite. Now, here in the clinic, it does indeed sound foolish. Yet, I certainly knew these things before kidney failure. Quantum mechanics is about measurement. The philosophic innovations that come out of it have to do with measurement and the problem of using physical concepts developed on this level to describe atomic events—uncertainty, probability, the "complementarity" of waves and particles were concepts useful on the subatomic level. This was the basis of Niels Bohr's Copenhagen Interpretation of Quantum Mechanics. All that stuff about consciousness and the universe resembling a great thought—or Brahman, atman, whatever—was never physics. At most, it was wishful thinking. Observation, as used by a physicist, means recording data, usually indirectly through instruments; observation includes theory, experimental methods, relevant data. In physics, observation is something we say about nature. Again, proof by potency.

Now, I feel sadness laced with anger. Madonna, Oprah, Deepak, they are masters of facile truths, of deception, and the bloodless, inoffensive banalities, making all struggles soft and easy—they are masters of the lazy person's thinking kit. Is everyone comfortable? Why, someone like Solzhenitsyn would wither them with a glance.

The nurse, ironically the one also named Madonna, pulls my needles. The venous needle comes out painfully and I bleed extra hard from that wound.

Meanwhile, on television, Madonna has been replaced by *The Price Is Right*.

∾

Some Eastern philosophies hold that with great effort one is capable of one's own salvation. This resembles the ancient theological battle between St. Augustine and Pelagius—Augustine emerged victorious with the doctrine of Original Sin. Ultimately, human beings are deeply flawed and incapable of saving themselves. And so in the West a savior is required: Jesus, Marx, Oprah, Deepak. Naturally, popular religion in the East had its avatars, incarnations, bodhisattvas. In theory at least they act as models. We, the tragic choir, need to do the difficult work. Western religion too often becomes something of a spectator sport or a reading assignment. Alan Watts said that Western religion was like going to a restaurant and eating the menu.

But here come the popularizers: The East is good; the West is bad. The East has the answers; the West has only its chronic and continual perplexities, which are unsolvable because they aren't *real* perplexities—if a question is unanswerable it really isn't a question. And so don't climb the Buddha's ladder, but create your own and pull it up after you. My friend Yakob and I would debate these issues, and we never reached a conclusion. And only later did I see, as it is said in Zen, no conclusion is the conclusion.

It's mid-January and late afternoon; the world has fallen into the violet half-light of a winter dusk. Out running, my arm burning and my legs feeling as if they're encased in concrete, I am thinking about Eastern philosophy. In a week I'll be teaching it to a college class.

It's a struggle to run today. I'm saddened by the disaster of my toxin-saturated flesh. Only Misha the malamute, who loves the winter, keeps me going. He's a Zen dog. He runs without a goal. Misha does have Buddha nature.

There sits Zukav, smiling. Oprah, Madonna, too. They begin to sound like the Grand Inquisitor Dostoevsky knew so well, giving us authority, mystery, and miracle. They make what is difficult far too easy.

Every step feels worse, every mile slower than the last.

But such things need to be difficult. The crucial test of any of our modern saviors would be to come back to their works, time and time again, and find sustenance and surprise. We require only those gods that give us the strength to face what is most hard in life.

I struggle through the run. It is still a joy to be alive and out running on a cold winter's day.

A Friday in the second week of January—only two sticks and I ran on the machine like a deer, as the nurses say.

Suddenly one of the patients sitting two chairs away— Leon, aged sixty with diabetes and a bad heart—awakens from a deep sleep; a sleep so deep that he never even stirred when they took his blood pressure. But now he is brought out of his dreams by the sound of the patient voices.

He looks up, apparently believing that the voices are coming from the television. It's Oprah again. She's smiling benignly, talking incessantly, thankfully without sound.

Leon raises his arms toward the glow.

The abrupt motion dislodges his arterial needle. In an instant blood shoots across the room. A number of patients—including me—call for the nurses. They're on break.

Thoroughly confused, Leon tries to rise from his chair. The other needle, the venous one, pulls out. There's blood everywhere.

Finally, the nurses arrive—Peggy, Vicki, Madonna. They hover over Leon and I can't see what's happening.

But the blood flow has ceased. I'm fairly sure he will live to be stuck another day.

I glance up. Oprah's still on the screen and hasn't noticed a thing. She's wearing a tight black sweater. The people sitting around her are weeping. I never find out why.

# ⮚ 14 ⮘

# Compassion

(DANTE, INFERNO, CANTO 16)

Another Monday morning and Nurse Nancy is ask-ing about my weekend. She is a large, heavy-boned woman, a decade younger, who's always smiling. I think she'd still smile even if I yelled obscenities into her face.

Marginally employed, a professor, weekends are not much different from weekdays, I joke. She doesn't even laugh but launches off on her own adventures: shopping, movies, TV, parties—especially parties.

Meanwhile, she completely misses my access with the second stick. Now I have a huge hema-tomato.

"Let me talk to Big Daddy," I plead, upset and in pain.

Big Daddy, however, is nowhere to be found, so they send in the social worker. She's always cheery and sooth-ing, prepared to listen to my problems, and bury me under more therapy.

Therapy, I've come to learn, is an attitude toward life: Either the disturbances within are due to forces beyond me, be they genetics, past events, outside powers, or, my "beliefs" about such things need changing. It is the cure-all of the welfare state. But, I am not encouraged to be strong and laugh in the face of my suffering, to be courageous in my misery, or, on the other hand, "to rage against the night." Oh no.

She opens with a diversion obviously designed to get me out of my ego cocoon: "What'd you think about Clinton?"

The screens above are filled with his guilty face leering down upon the crucified.

I give a slight shrug, which is all the tubes permit. "Means little. Background noise . . . less than that, to tell the truth."

As if she hasn't heard a word, she launches into an analysis of his excessive need to be loved.

Kafka again: "For the last time psychology!"

Maybe I quote Kafka aloud because she's frowning, and she hardly ever frowns. With the fluid shifts, the strain of treatment on the body, the overall loss of control, I find myself slipping, giving voice to thoughts that should remain unsaid.

"How about him?" She asks again.

"Who?"

"The President!"

"Irrelevant."

"But don't you think we need values? Morals?"

"We do? You know, I've struggled with chaos math for years. Still struggle. But one thing I've learned is how much our culture hates and fears uncertainty, the frightful randomness of things. It's the old Greek problem. We'll always take Plato over Heraclitus. We want Platonic values, absolute, unchanging guides, like some moral map. But the contingent frailty of things in this world offends us. So we imagine some other world of perfection, changelessness, heaven, and we set it over the real world and suffer because they never truly intersect. . . ."

I clap my mouth shut. This is far too much. Her smile has long since departed, replaced by a look of sincere worry. No doubt, she's going through a mental list of professional therapists she might call. But given the clinic's budget, such resources are scarce. And I'm thankful.

"What about President Pudd?" Pudd is my new name for Clinton.

"Yes?" She sounds relieved. I'm back to reality.

"I'll tell you a story. The father and brothers of St. Thomas Aquinas locked him in a castle tower in order to prevent him from becoming a Dominican monk. A prisoner, he spent his time in prayer and meditation. They quickly saw that they'd failed.

"Next they sent a beautiful Neapolitan prostitute to seduce St. Thomas. She'd barely stepped into the tower, when St. Thomas seized a burning branch from the fireplace and thrust it at her, yelling for her to get out. Naturally, she fled, screaming that he was a wild man. He even burned the door and lock behind her.

"After this event his father and brothers relented and agreed that he become a Dominican.

"President Pudd could have taken *that* lesson from St. Thomas."

On to the next patient, she surrenders my miserable corpse to the depression demons—therapy for the damned.

I'm fighting to prevent this illness from consuming me. I watched it happen to my father. He became his own tiny solar system, molding his life so that the smallest detail revolved around the routine of sickness, and inflating his ego to absurd proportions.

Then along comes therapy, talking about self-love. Real therapy needs to set self-love aside.

But they are all on the side of the sick, shielding us from this sort of struggle. They claim to drag us out of our illness syndrome. I think the opposite occurs. Struggling and depressed, I begin to grasp at a gut level the struggle of others, the cancer patients, the victims of disasters, accidents, crimes—suffering. *Compassion* slowly begins to grow within me; like the lotus plant with its roots in the mud it rises to the surface, and I begin to feel better. A student once complained to his Zen master that he was discouraged with his practice. "Encourage others," said the master.

My brain is soaked in toxins, they say. Therapy always wins.

I smile sadly and glance up at the screen. Now it's Starr, then Hyde, then back to Starr. All without sound.

Lucky for Bill, buggery is not one of his appetites. Imagine Starr peering up that breech? Oh Rabelais, how we need you!

Too bad Rabelais is not a TV anchor.

# ❧ 15 ❧

# What Ails You, Father?

(DANTE, INFERNO, CANTO 33)

Today Momma Cass asks me again if I'd rather go to the evening shift where she's working.

"Can't," I repeat, "parental responsibilities."

She shrugs. "I understand."

I wonder what my children understand. Of my three children, only the oldest, my sixteen-year-old son Luc, has any real memories of a healthy father, a father who could romp, tumble, and play, a father with enough energy to take an active role in his life. With the others, two girls, Sophia and Anna, fatherhood has become a spectator sport. In the bleak summer of 1998, resisting dialysis, my eleven-year-old Sophia blurted out one day, "Daddy, when will you die?"

Dr. Jung warned me repeatedly that the body adjusts to high toxin levels, so slowly that the patient usually doesn't notice. I discovered on my own that this is also true of personality, of character in general.

A morose and thick blanket of gloom settled over our home. The smallest events irritated me; normal childhood behavior triggered rages, tirades, or mean-spirited comments. Often the causes were forgotten while the anger festered like the toxins my kidneys could not clear.

Anger is poison, said the Buddha, another truth I had forgotten because of the chemical poisons in my blood.

The vented rages would be followed by profound remorse. Deep-set loathing and self-disgust overwhelmed me. It was as if I could suddenly see through a blinding fog—the anger, the rages, were over nothing. The Buddhist sutras did no good. Anger is poison, they shouted into my ears. Yet, I'd grown deaf. Only self-loathing made me see clearly. Another one for depression.

It was frightening. My personality was changing and there seemed to be nothing I could do to stop it. Even more frightening was the tiny voice that whispered perhaps this was my true self, my real personality coming out.

In those moments of apparent lucidity, in the depths of melancholia, I mentioned leaving, going away somewhere to live in isolation and spare those I loved the pain. Such statements, uttered out of frustration, provoked bouts of weeping from Sophia. Five-year-old Anna could hardly comprehend, and Luc acted predictably: He left.

And in those moments, perceiving the damage I'd inflicted, I truly wished to disappear. Death wish, Thanatos. This, too, may have contributed to the crazy postponement of dialysis.

∼

With blood pressure under control, due to a combination of medication and dialysis, toxins somewhat lower, the rages and black depression have subsided. Yet, at moments when they still flutter inside, like bats at dusk, I am left feeling hopeless, standing like a spectator unable to exert the slightest influence. Actor, spectator, both at the same time, body chemistry writes the screenplay.

Momma Cass moves on, tending to the other patients. These memories are more painful than a hundred sticks! What damage has my illness done to my own children? I glance up at the screen; nothing but Clinton and endless replays of his troubles.

Does no one remember that crazed villain the Marquis Donatien Alphonse-Francois de Sade? He wrote many of his books while in prison; one, written in 1785, was titled *Les 120 Journées des Sodome*. Here the good marquis asks the priests, the moralists, the lawmakers: "you tonsured riffraff"—in my language the therapists—what will become of your sins and punishments once it has been shown "that this or that current of fluid, or a certain grain, or degree of acidity in the blood or the juices will suffice to subjugate men . . . ?" What if self-control—morality—is nothing more than the "degree of acidity in the blood?"

And yet, thinking back, I realize that at times I won the battle, controlled my emotions, and acted with compassion and dignity despite the "degree of acidity" in my toxic blood.

Meditation truly healed only when directed toward its authentic task (as I "remembered" from the Buddhist sutras): the realization that the absolute self is an *illusion*. *There is no such thing as a permanent self, a soul, an absolute identity*, the doctrine of no-self (*anatman*). Anger is poison secreted from this false idea of an absolute self.

Such is the central message of the ancient writings. Not self-help, not Deepak's longevity, not Oprah and Madonna's soft salvation; rather the hard, nearly impossible task of detachment from self and its cravings. This is the doctrine of *anatman*, no-self, which arises from the major premise that all conditioned things are transitory—*anicca*.

The thought of impermanence exercised a calming effect. Meditating on the transitory nature of self, the past became unreal, the memories that build self melted away, and the future, now in doubt, faded into nothingness.

One must bring mindfulness into the daily habits of simple living. Meditation is not enough, like trying to make a mirror by rubbing two stones together, as a Zen master once taught an overzealous student. One meditates on the impermanence of self and for a brief moment is able to detach from the self's insistent cravings. Afterward, one is tossed back into the daily activities of life, which fortify self like impenetrable stone and mortar. Yet, these very daily activities are possessed of a dignity and value all their own: the routine chores, the chit-chat, the loafing, meals, off-hand jests, so many tiny and precious things one is hardly aware of until chronic illness takes them away, or simply doing them becomes a major effort of will. And yet again, should one destroy cravings, attachments, one would destroy capitalism. Without self and its desires, constantly aroused, infinitely expanded, capitalism would languish in empty and futile gestures. True healing for the therapists, Deepak, Oprah, would be financial death.

Still, the crazy marquis had a point. Character, personality, spontaneous behavior are not fully ours to control. Unconscious forces, some chemical and others not, pull us this way and that. The strength of our shining consciousness is no more than a spider's web stretched thin. Only on the calmest, sunniest days does the pattern hold. But the rain and wind soon wash it away.

Who understood such hard truths better than Nietzsche? He warned against the error of mistaking cause for consequence, the error of imaginary causes, the error of false causality. The causes of behavior are so complex and myriad that even the largest computer could not catalogue them: language, culture, the physical environment, "the degree of acidity in the blood." And what, then, Monsieur l'Abbé, asks the crazy marquis, of your sin? Of guilt?

Biologist G. G. Simpson once called genetic disposition "the result of a purposeless and natural process that did not have (us) in mind."

I'm sitting very quietly in my chair, nearing the end of treatment, struggling with these thoughts. I dare not utter a word. They are disquieting, dangerous, perplexing ideas, and perhaps unsolvable to our species, at least now in our evolution. I glance up. Perhaps it's better to have no-brain Madonna jabber on about spiritual urges and Oprah bless us.

Any explanation is better than no explanation, says Nietzsche, who himself made good medicine from his own chronic illness.

~

After a great deal of coaxing and pressure—the campaign conducted by an alliance of Dr. Jung and my wife—I finally stepped into *her* office, February 1998. It's in the other wing of the clinic building, a few miles from the hospital. This was the first time I even acknowledged the existence of the dialysis clinic.

I shall call her Samantha. She is the dialysis clinic coordinator for new patient education. Her job is coaxing. It was her task to apply all of her talents—and they are considerable—to convince me that I needed help. Help, of course, meant dialysis.

Her first assignment was to get me to submit to surgery on my right forearm—preparing an access for the dialysis needles. This is, as previously mentioned, the fistula, created by shunting an artery into a vein. As noted earlier, prior to 1960, dialysis access usually meant a new vein and artery for every treatment. Vessels were quickly used up. Someone with chronic renal failure ultimately died. Then, in 1960, Belding Scribner and Wayne Quinton created an external arterial to venous shunt, using tubing designed for electrical conduit. The first shunt was implanted in the arm of Clyde Shields. Problems resulted from infection and the rigid design of the shunt irritating the vessels. Finally, James Cimino perfected the internal fistula, making it possible to treat kidney failure indefinitely.

Yet, I resisted. Such an operation would be tangible proof that I'd started down the road blazed by my father.

But ill, fatigued, depressed, shivering in the February chill, I was no match for Sam's smooth persuasiveness and long experience. In a week, all resistance collapsed, the battle conceded with hardly a skirmish. I submitted to surgery.

During our discussions, Sam told me an interesting story. She said:

"Many patients, sitting there in your seat, break down and cry when it finally hits them that they're in renal failure. I try to get them to accept it. [*Acceptance*, the word for 1998; a word I've since forgotten because, looking back, I realize I still don't accept this!] After a time they do. They accept their kidney failure and the realization that we can help.

"But then they go back to their rural communities and talk to their ministers. Their ministers and the entire congregation pray for them, and they pray to Jesus. And still their kidneys fail.

"So, the minister tells them that their *faith in Jesus isn't strong enough*, otherwise their kidneys wouldn't fail. The whole church knows it too. And the poor patient reverts back to misery, now laced with guilt."

I sigh and quote Nietzsche: "Even chance—the randomness of illness, of genetics—Christianity robs chance of its innocence!"

Better, however, is the Buddha's story about the arrow wound:

> A man has been wounded by an arrow thickly smeared with poison. As his kinsfolk seek to procure a physician, what if this wounded one were to say: "I will not have this arrow removed until I have learned whether the man who wounded me belonged to the warrior caste, or the Brahman; or whether the arrow itself was iron or stone; or whether this man came from a village or city, or whether he was black, white, or yellow . . . Now, said the Buddha, don't such questions already add mental suffering to the grief that's already poisoning the flesh? One must pull out the arrow.

And this, I add, was the task of the Buddha: to extract the arrow of suffering, not add mental anguish like so much salad dressing. Not to add guilt for weak faith.

Samantha nodded. But then Samantha agreed with everything I said in those days; it was her job.

Later that same day, I was teaching a class on the history of the Medieval Church. The subject was the German mystic Meister Eckhart. I noticed a student with a rainbow watchband, golden letters embroidered upon it: WWJD.

After class, I teased her about the meaning of the letters.

"What Would Jesus Do? I always ask myself."

"Good question! But who will ever know?"

"One must have faith," she answered with quiet certainty.

"Yes," I agreed and walked back to my office, exhausted as always.

Let her have her Jesus. But I hope that her Jesus is of the species that pulls out arrows.

~

A note:

It is the end of January 1999, a Monday morning. The Denver Broncos have just won the Super Bowl. The players, interviewed on morning television (as I'm stuck with the damned needles) are praising God and Jesus, implying that Jesus himself took an active hand in the game, in the actual running, tackling, catching, throwing. Divine intervention. The interviewer, some famous morning personality, obviously agrees.

Jesus is apparently more concerned about football than the legions of the suffering, than, say, childhood cancer, genocide, starvation, or end-stage renal failure. Jesus lets such obscenities pass, but he passes footballs and intervenes directly to alter the course of the game!

And such absurdities merit discussion and the attention of the press. Why not start off the morning talking about Kierkegaard (fear and trembling)? Or old Schopenhauer contemplating the cholera epidemic of 1832: " . . . this world could not be the work of an all-loving Being, but rather that of a devil, who had brought creatures into existence in order to delight in the sight of their sufferings."

No. Jesus scoring a touchdown, Jesus making a jump shot go in the hoop.

Naturally, my mind is poisoned with toxins, which explains why I think such foolish things about the Super Bowl.

# ⁓ 16 ⁓

# Prophecy

(DANTE, INFERNO, CANTO 15)

Until December 1997, when my creatinine was nearing ten, I firmly believed that meditation was working and my kidneys were healing. Didn't Deepak say that
the universe was a great thought?

The universe may be a great thought (or it may not
be), but it is not *my thought*. Deepak advised to find the
space between thoughts. Such gaps, he claimed, are
"fields of infinite possibilities." Consciousness, therefore,
conceives, constructs and becomes the physical body.

In truth, it was Sir James Jeans who said that the universe was a great thought, and he was speaking metaphor-
ically, referring to the fact that in modern physics, natural
law had dissolved into abstract mathematics. Deepak,
like all fundamentalists, was taking metaphor literally. In
the present culture, this sort of breathless thinking pays
handsomely.

Or, could it be we no longer live in a culture; we live
in a massive department store?

⁓

When does optimism become denial? When does accep-tance become destiny?

I'd force myself to be active; I sought out more stress and work, more time with the kids, teaching, running, researching, planning vast projects, as if to prove the numbers wrong. Numbers are statistical truths. Why not simply ignore the numbers? I'm feeling fine. I'm going about my affairs.

But it wasn't true. Armine could see clearly the gradual decline. I refused to believe her. I even ignored her increas-ing habit of dissolving into tears at the slightest mention of my illness. I believed that it was her problem, not mine. The arguments mounted in frequency and intensity. Our marriage was becoming a fragmented, jumbled puzzle with pieces strewn all about, some lost for good.

That damned bad feeling just creeps a slow inch at a time, and then suddenly one is in a valley wondering why the heights are so distant. Feeling good, or even decent, is a faded memory. One takes feeling bad as normal.

∼

In March 1998, I went into the hospital for a transplant evaluation. Less evaluation and more like five hours of the modern inquisition, I lost more blood than one of Dracula's victims. I made the joke numerous times during the day, several times to the same people. It was like a bad joke contest, theirs against mine.

I went through a psyche evaluation—actually, a few questions about whether I'd continue working on dialy-sis. Apparently, my professorial status convinced them of my mental stability. Fortunately, they never asked any of my former students.

Now came more bad news: The work-up had revealed a defective heart valve. The long years of high blood pressure, coupled with the stress of distance running, had turned my mitral valve into a floppy, leaky mess. Once again, there were no symptoms; my body had adjusted to the defect.

The next day was surgery to create the fistula, the dialysis access, so it would be matured when the time came. But I still don't believe that the time will come, this rainy March of 1998.

The procedure is called Same Day Surgery. I arrived at six in the morning and got into that ridiculous hospital gown that opens in the back. Eventually, I was on the stretcher waiting in the anteroom. They'd inserted an IV. The wait was more than an hour.

At last, I got wheeled into the operating room, which was dominated by massive, mirror-like lights. It was extremely cold and severe. I struggled not to look at the surgical instruments. The surgeon, a man I'd met previously, began making small talk—actually, large talk—asking me about the history of physics, about Einstein, Bohr, the twentieth century revolution. Nervous—no, scared silly—I foolishly launched into a lecture, cut off mid-sentence when the anesthesiologist opened a valve, probably at a subtle signal from the bored surgeon. Too bad students are not able to do such a thing. Higher education would be so much more enjoyable.

~

I opened my eyes. Armine was there, hovering over me. The painfully bright lights had vanished. It seemed as if only a few seconds had passed. In fact, it had been two hours. This had to be the blackest, most dreamless of all sleeps. No lights, no tunnels, no hovering over the operating table, no saints, virgin mothers, or Hebrew saviors, no buddhas, no Krishnas, no Deepaks. Nothing.

Then I felt the burning in my right forearm. Quickly, they pumped something into the IV and immediately my body became numb, perception uncertain. The mad marquis was right, the proper chemicals—"a certain grain"—manipulate us like puppets.

The arm healed nicely. I was left with a two inch scar on my wrist immediately below the thumb. But in the first days of recovery, I suffered a terrible case of constipation. This experience proved far worse than surgery. It took more drugs to relieve the problem. In the meantime, I became nearly scatological, obsessed with my bowels.

I can well believe Erikson's analysis of Father Martin Luther. Father Martin, suffering painful constipation, found relief not in drugs but in theology. His great theological breakthrough—and relief did indeed feel like a breakthrough—came in the *cloacha*, the privy. After that, he refused to compromise. Hence the birth of Protestantism, and, if Weber is to be believed, capitalism as well.

I gained a new empathy for Martin Luther and the sacred nature of defecation, which no philosophy has truly considered.

∾

I now had my fistula. By April of 1998, it had matured and was ready to be used. The creatinine inched upwards. Then, in mid-April, it actually dropped a point. Ha! Proof! I was right to resist! Naturally, I ignored the fact that I'd had a touch of stomach flu and had neither eaten nor run for a week.

I stubbornly held out, despite the destruction of other organs (the mitral valve) and the poisoning of my marriage.

I still hoped for a miracle. I'd studied the philosophy and history of science. I knew the great, yawning chasms of our knowledge, the limits of rationalism. Now, during this spring, I dropped Deepak's methods (or lack thereof) and came back to Zen. It would happen. "Form is emptiness, emptiness is not different from form, neither is form different from emptiness, indeed emptiness is form." The famous words of the *Prajna Paramita Hridaya Sutra* (The Heart Sutra of Perfect Wisdom). I may have taken up Zen, but for all the wrong reasons. Hence, it was not Zen. No one takes up Zen. Taking up Zen is not taking up Zen. One does not pick it off the ground like a stone; look, here it is, look, there it goes.

Daffy (my new name, close enough to Deepak) believed, however, *a miracle would happen!* The body is an expression of the mind . . . the universe is a great thought . . . miracles.

Then I went to Hawaii.

# ⭐ 17 ⭐

## Fool's Flight

(DANTE, INFERNO, CANTO 26)

I met a medical school professor who's had a transplanted kidney for twenty years. Twenty years ago, he told me, dialysis was absolutely primitive. Kolff's kidney was a huge rotating drum, using sausage skin for the dialyzing membrane. A later machine, the Kiil dialyzer, used parallel plates bolted together with a cellulose membrane. Leaks, breakdowns, poor dialysis, were common. Cleaning and maintaining the machine meant nearly rebuilding it before each treatment. Until the late 1970s and capillary flow dialyzers (portable cylinders stuffed with tiny fibers) dialysis was a full time operation—six hours on, six hours to clean and reassemble. I shudder.

"Did you experience denial?" I ask him.

He laughs. "The month before I went on dialysis, I took a trip to Lapland. I got better on a diet of yogurt."

Lapland. My Lapland was Hawaii.

In May of 1998, Armine and I went to Hawaii for three weeks. Had this trip been filmed, say, as a National Geographic Travel Special, it would have been titled *Nauseated by Paradise*.

Why did I do such a daffy thing? I asked the medical school professor this very question about Lapland, and he gave me an incredulous smile as if to say: "Don't you know?"

Dr. Jung wanted me to start dialysis. My creatinine edged over twelve, my BUN near two hundred. It was an awful risk. "You don't get a medal for suffering," he said.

Why? The obvious reason is—as my Lapland buddy would have said—*escape*. I said that I wanted to visit a certain Zen monastery. I wanted to restore our marriage. It would be one last trip, to talk to the monks, to experience Zen once again, not out of books.

The Buddha would have said I was trying to escape the person who shot the arrow. That person happened to be my own genes. Perhaps, too, I was looking for salvation some*place* much as Christians search for salvation in some*one*.

But we carry our doom with us, either to the islands or into the cathedral. Traveling makes heavy demands on the healthiest person. Exotic cuisine (not yogurt!) can upset the best digestions; jet lag can drain the most energetic of people.

One day on Oahu, I tried to run from our hotel to Diamond Head, about six miles. I forced myself to run fast (actually, it was only the illusion of speed). I finished in a near faint. That evening we dined in an open-air restaurant on a beach, as perfect as a dream. Except I could not eat! Not a bite. The smell alone drove me to the point of retching. To this day, I cannot recall the food, whether it was pork, fish, lamb.

We flew to Kauai, the garden island. Nausea and fatigue flew with me. We went snorkeling, seventy miles up the Na Pali Coast. I became seasick (I had grown up on Lake Michigan around boats, on the open water). Bobbing in gentle waves, I vomited breakfast, scrambled eggs, around three in the afternoon.

Brilliantly colored reef fish, absent till this moment, suddenly appeared in thick schools to feast. Kidney failure fed the fish.

On the boat, I suffered convulsions and terrible cold. The salty spray, the rolling, the pounding waves . . . at one point, still miles from the harbor, I firmly believed that the end had come. This feeling came as relief.

But I survived. Back in our hotel, sweating beneath a pile of blankets in the tropics, the nausea finally passed. Outside, I could hear laughter drifting up from the beach: music, excited voices, eating, drinking—a party. Life.

It left me cold.

A few days later, we kayaked four miles up the Waimea River on Kauai. I had recovered. Nothing but a case of seasickness, I said. Four miles of constant paddling had me gasping for air. In a lovely inlet, we tied the kayak and hiked another five miles through tropical rain forest to a waterfall. During our hike, it rained three times. The ground became muddy, slippery. My knees and ankles ached and creaked like rusty hinges hundreds of years old (later I would learn that the buildup of phosphorus, yet another reward for avoiding dialysis, causes the joints to grind and freeze). At one point I passed into paranoid delusion, thinking Armine was trying to kill me on the slippery trail and collect the insurance. We made it to the waterfall. Even the most spectacular natural beauty could not distract physical misery. Somehow—a true miracle— I stumbled and slid back to the kayak. We paddled farther up that endless river to a fern grotto. Unable to pull myself out of the kayak, I waited for Armine. Feeling old and worn-out, and useless, I was quite prepared to welcome death. Dying would be a gentle relief.

Finally, we started back, toward the mouth of the river and the ocean. We paddled up current, against a stiff wind. Once more, I believed the end had come, and was thankful.

Back on the island of Oahu, I visited a Zen monastery located in mountain foothills, serene and beautiful. The monks were cordial, mostly smiling at my questions. They watched me with soft eyes, knowingly, sensing, perhaps, the death oozing from my pores. I wandered the grounds and discovered a meditation house built on a small, gushing mountain stream. Tiny cups filled with water, spilled over and filled the next, so on down, setting off clappers. Meditating, I noticed that the clappers seemed to match the cadence of normal breathing. I practiced too, for some time.

The thought came to me as I sat surrounded by the mountain, the stream, the Asian architecture, and even the huge statue of Buddha seated in meditation having passed beyond samsara, the wheel of suffering, that just maybe, in this setting, I actually could have healed my decayed kidneys.

On the plane home, I noticed that my ankles had swollen to the size of my calves. Before the 1820s, physicians would have called my disease dropsy. Any time bloating due to excess fluid appeared, the disease was dropsy. Boswell describes Samuel Johnson's suffering the floods of water in his flesh. Autopsy revealed both cardiac and renal disease. In the nineteenth century, Richard Bright recognized the uremic symptoms of renal failure, how many patients had albumin in their urine (which he detected by heating the urine in a spoon with a candle to coagulate the protein), how many were deficient in urine. Thus, renal failure became Bright's Disease until the twentieth century.

Flying east created a day without end. Somehow, I endured. After a week's rest at home, I began to feel better. Nothing but the rigors of traveling, I told myself. But the edema persisted. Nineteenth century physicians would have known what I refused to acknowledge.

~

No one knows how much the toxins affect the higher mental processes—for that matter, the lower ones! The doctors can only guess. I noticed that my short-term memory was leaking. My wife and kids would tell me things in the morning, which I would forget in the afternoon, and then in the evening accuse them of not telling me. It became a vicious circle, spinning out of control.

I tried to do scholarly work that terrible summer of 1998. But my concentration was good for an hour at best. I was supposed to be on sabbatical, producing scholarship. Most of my days were spent in desultory reading.

Despite the numbers, I created fascinating interpretations, or I simply ignored them with goofy philosophical arguments. For example, Godel's incompleteness theorem: Mathematics cannot account for its own foundations, therefore I am not required by logic to accept numbers as meaningful. I could have written entire books on "The Refutation of Modern Medicine", or "Physician Heal Thyself, and Leave Me Alone;" better might have been: "My Flesh Is Weak—and So Is My Mind."

June came. No dialysis.

# ❧ 18 ❧

# Love

(DANTE, INFERNO, CANTO 5)

Every day free from dialysis was a day of hope. Maybe today the healing would begin. Perhaps in this very moment the spiraling decline would be reversed. But once I started dialysis it would be all over. Defeat would be certain.

Therefore, I held out through July and August. One weekend Dr. Jung asked for a collection of urine. The results were predictable: My kidneys were barely functioning. I was given Lasix to help pass the excess fluid. One morning I noticed abdominal swelling. My ankles remained puffy, like bread dough. Running became ever more difficult; just stepping out the door was a test of will. The summer heat made running tough, I told myself.

Avoiding dialysis was rational, I said. Meditation practice requires patience.

Armine began to exhibit signs of the strain with uncontrollable weeping; she became angry, then gloomy. I told her that I was feeling better and she laughed bitterly.

And yet, the Buddhist sutras were whispering to me: One must expect illness, accidents, pain, as conditions of life, evidence if not proof of the central doctrine of impermanence. One must expect and learn from them. Even the Buddha died.

I was struggling to freeze my vision, my memory, of a healthy self. But the sutras kept saying that the permanent self was an illusion built from sensation, perception (giving meaning to sensation), memory, anticipation—in short, attachments. This ego, this seemingly changeless thing called self, or soul, body or mind or both, was like a blazing torch, consuming, being consumed.

> All the world is on fire,
>
> All the world is burning,
>
> All the world is ablaze,
>
> All the world is quaking.
>
> —Bhikkunisamyutta, 542

I studied the concept of *Shunyata* in depth from Nagarjuna's second century c.e. *Mulamadhyamakakarika*. *Shunyata* means emptiness, though not the emptiness of Western philosophy. In Buddhism, *Shunyata* carries a positive meaning: Everything changes, everything is in motion, and is dependently arising. All composite things, my kidneys included, arise from conditions: genetics, environment, diet, work. Yet, these things are not themselves the static causes of effects for they too arise from conditions and are in a continual state of flux. Dr. Jung explained that even normal kidneys declined with age. All conditioned things are destined to pass away in time. All that exists possesses no inherent or permanent characteristics by which the thing may be described or absolutely defined. Everything is changing from instant to instant, and no observer is privileged, absolutely stable.

Yet, this vision of reality is not distressing; one does not despair. It is called *pratitya-samutpada*, the doctrine of dependent origination (or interdependent conditioning). It says that this self, these kidneys, these lungs, this heart, intestines, hair, and skin—these memories, anticipations, hopes, beliefs, personality—are all like an image described by the nineteenth century Indian saint Sri Ramakrishna: Here is a salt doll or statue, a figure made from salt. Throw the creature into the sea. What remains? The great salt ocean. This self is empty, empty of unchanging characteristics, empty of stability, empty of *constant health*.

This vision, ironically, did infinitely more for me than any practice. I began to see, as the Zen monk Thich Nhat Hanh once said, that we are "inter-are" with the rest of existence. Impermanence is reason for hope. Instead of looking at things falsely, from the narrow, suffering self, with the proper discipline I could see myself in these clouds that give this rain that grows these crops that sustain all life, my life too, failed kidneys and all. With no permanent self, *I am these causes and conditions*, and they too are impermanent, empty of "self." With this vision of reality, truly could I become free from fear and anger, compassionate.

> Bhikkhus, form is impermanent. The cause and
>
> condition for the arising of form is also
>
> impermanent. As form has originated from
>
> what is impermanent, how could it be
>
> permanent?
>
> —Khandhavagga, 18(7)

August 1998. What I was at that moment—nauseated, sick, weak, kidneys failing—seemed fleeting and intangible. Each morning I expected to awaken from the bad dream. What I was—strong, filled with energy, running marathons—appeared fixed and therefore tangible. But the past is vanished, never to return. It no longer exists. I tried to identify myself with that past, and hence with nonexistence. I projected that nonexistence into the future, which itself does not exist. I tried to live in those nonexistent time dimensions. But I did not *live*. . . .

I wished to heal. Healing became a craving; craving led to attachment; attachment reinforced the delusion of permanent self, and the self suffered. But nothing, health included, remains stable, standing outside contingency like some honored guest to life. The objects of desire are illusions when they are conceived as unchanging. I desired healthy kidneys, but all things are part of an all-consuming fire, reduced to ashes and smoke in time. I was that fire and smoke.

According to this philosophy, I was in a worse denial than any Western therapist could imagine. I was practicing meditation for all the wrong reasons. No wonder it didn't work.

One day I came across this passage in Philip Kapleau's *Three Pillars of Zen*:

> An ancient Zen saying has it that to become attached to one's own enlightenment is as much a sickness as to exhibit a maddeningly active ego. Indeed, the profounder the enlightenment, the worse the illness.

To preach no-self and nonattachment in our economy would be more revolutionary than Marxism. Such a one would never be "guru to the stars."

A book I came to love during that awful summer was one I picked up in the islands: poems of Zen Masters written at the moment of death.

Banzan, who died in 1730, wrote:

Farewell—

I pass as all things do

dew on the grass.

And Chogo, who died in 1806:

I long for people—

then again I loathe them;

end of autumn.

Kiba, who died in 1868, wrote:

My old body:

a drop of dew grown

heavy at the leaf tip.

My favorite is Moriya Sen'an:

Bury me when I die

beneath a wine barrel

in a tavern.

With luck

the cask will leak.

~

Late one August night, I found a talk show featuring Deepak Chopra. There was a question and answer period. A member of the audience asked the Master if he'd ever had a bad day.

Deepak gives his well-practiced smile and answered: "I never have a bad day."

Later, I watched an old movie with Anthony Quinn, who plays a Berber chief fighting the Italian fascists. The chief was captured and executed in the end. Mounting the scaffold, he prayed: "Thanks be to Allah for granting me my death at the hands of my enemies."

Deepak and I parted company that night. And as we parted, I joined the Beatles and sang over my shoulder: "Nothing is real and nothing to get hung about. Strawberry fields forever."

Thanks be to Allah for these bad days of kidney failure.

~

How could I have been daffy enough to fall for such stuff? How can one judge with a pickled brain that one's brain is pickled? Kidney failure too has a hermeneutic circle.

One night in early December of 1997, I was giving a public lecture on the Jesus Seminar, which is a contemporary association of scholars in search of the historical Jesus. Conservative faithful find these scholars quite shocking. Some, I imagine, would consign them to the lowest level of the pit, and have probably lobbied the deity for such a ruling. It was a Thursday evening, which meant that I'd already been teaching all day. Now I was talking again, to a packed audience of one hundred for nearly two hours. I was exhausted.

No sooner had the final word slipped from my mouth—the last thought from my toxic brain—a member of the audience arose and sprang to the attack. A philosophy professor, obviously a literalist, he'd been taking copious notes the entire time. Everything I'd said was completely wrong. My numbers were lies. My analyses were silly. My historical knowledge was nonexistent. Even my jokes stunk. The whole thing was an outrage: He was outraged that this passed for history. I was outrageous. I was out to destroy Christianity.

Normally I would have laughed and ridiculed his dishonesty, his attempt to count tiny papyrus fragments as entire manuscripts. I would have joked about the naiveté of thinking that any source has not been redacted, many times. Yet, this night my brain yielded no reply, and I waited patiently, absorbing every last drop of venom (which probably made little difference to my poisoned flesh), wanting only to go home to bed.

Once more, it was obvious that something was seriously wrong. I told myself that I'd had a long day. And, fortunately, other members of the audience joined in, defending my position. Well, I was allowing others to have their say.

Ironically, I don't necessarily accept the Jesus Seminar's version of the historical Jesus, a "Jewish Peasant" teaching a philosophy similar to the Greek Cynic philosophers. Double irony, I think this interpretation is an underhanded method of making Christianity palatable to moderns, thus rescuing it from the Enlightenment (David Hume) and the higher criticism. Blinded by their own literalism, fundamentalists cannot recognize a potential ally.

If my brain was pickled already in 1997, 1998 consigned it to the cellar.

∼

The middle of August 1998: I was getting worse. Coupled with almost daily nausea was a strong, metallic taste in my mouth that no toothpaste or mouthwash could dissolve. Running had become a three-mile stagger; this appeared to be the limits of my strength. I watched the news in a mental fog, wondering how President Pudd had the energy to fondle Monica.

At times, however, the fog lifted and I saw clearly what a fool I had become. And yet, every morning I looked for signs of healing.

A fool. In Italian, a fool is a *bizoccone*. Some fools, however, were holy fools, holy men wandering the dusty roads of medieval Italy. One holy fool was Jacopone da Todi who once said that the Incarnation was a mystery so deep that it would be better to pass over it. In the end, this seems to best summarize my own procrastination. When all the texts been scoured, all the denial words used up, all the rational and obvious explanations advanced, I still have the deepest gut feeling that something remains unsaid, some primal monster remains swimming far beneath the waves, and it would rip to shreds any conceptual net that tried to capture it.

But holy fools could be useful. When Russian Tsar Ivan IV (the Dread) left Novgorod, in February of 1570, having slaughtered its citizenry, he was confronted on the road by a holy fool, one Nickolay. Nickolay went naked in the Russian winter. He waved a bloody piece of meat beneath Ivan's nose and called him "Emperor Bloodsucker."

Then Nickolay said: "If you don't go home something terrible will happen to you."

At the very moment the holy fool finished speaking, a loud clap of thunder shook the countryside.

Ivan went home.

But I was just a fool. Oh for the wisdom of a holy fool!

∼

I still didn't believe I'd need dialysis. I was something like the contemporary fool in Max Picard's *The Flight from God*. In place of real fear—I could drop dead at any moment—was only an anxious pedantry—I was constantly looking for reasons to refuse treatment.

However, it also became depressingly easy to feel sorry for myself. Why, of all the people my age who go blithely walking through life, had this happened to me? It was easy to pass from self-pity into anger. It was even easier to project this anger outward onto others, onto my wife, my children. As I was dying, so, too, were my relationships. It was a frightful torture to see my anger projected and yet be unable to halt it. And in the background stood, unanswered, the question of the molecules. How much of this was due to the toxins flooding my brain?

I felt like the victim in the first volume of Solzhenitsyn's *Gulag Archipelago*. The chap is accused by his neighbor of some heinous crime against the state and he says to the judge: "But your honor, I did nothing!"

And the judge replies: "Ten years for doing nothing."
Of course the poor fool dies in Siberia.

Yet, such thoughts were like asking about the warrior who fired the poisoned arrow. I merely added mental anguish to physical pain, no different from those poor innocents told that their kidney failure is the result of their weak faith in Jesus.

It is the problem of the self. The self resists. Illness actually seems to inflate the ego. It becomes totally self-consumed, one-dimensional, and cocooned in the disease. Nothing in the world is powerful enough to divert attention from the self and its cravings.

But the self is an illusion, I kept repeating. Alas, to no avail. Slowly my meditation changed. No longer was I trying to *do* anything. Now I merely floated like some disembodied observer of the death process, watching the body, the self, slowly die.

∽

Late August: I can't eat or drink. I experienced stomach spasms the instant I ingested the smallest morsel of food. Intestinal pain, bloating, diarrhea . . . one at time, it seemed, my physical functions began to shut down, close up shop. Nothing in the world seemed interesting, nothing worth the effort. All the activity around me appeared futile and comical.

There's something else. Perhaps Socrates knew of it when, as the poison penetrated his cells, he requested that his friends pay his debt to Asceplius, the god of medicine. Life, Socrates seemed to be saying, is an illness and now it's over—pay the medical debt. This self was dying every moment and yet I did not notice. It was flowing, burning out, and all my desires to make of it a stasis, an unchanging thing, caused emotional and mental illness.

Again, I saw how the whole economic world was geared to preserving, indeed inflating this self. No wonder the central doctrine of Buddhism will never make it on television. But for me, as the lights went out in body and soul, the frenzied and ceaseless materialist cravings were revealed in all their duplicity.

What a dichotomy! Illness reinforces the self, while at the same time highlights its true nature, that it is illusion.

The last week of August: Armine and I sat out on the back deck. I'd just returned from a run. I was trying to convince her that today, at least, I felt better.

She began to cry.

I looked at her, really *looked* at her. She, a nurse, knew what was happening; she knew dialysis could help me. I saw her frustration, her suffering, the damage all this had done to her. I saw how everything in our twenty-two years together was collapsing. She had three children to raise. Her own parents divorced when she was six, and that was still a sharp pain. She was reliving the frightening insecurity of a child caught in a divorce with me in our marriage. Shortly I'd be gone. I saw it in her eyes. For a moment, the toxins released my brain and I saw how another, one I love, suffered. Perhaps the run cleared my mind for a few seconds, enough to see.

I get up and go into the house. I dialed Dr. Jung's number. "I'm ready for dialysis," I told him.

And so, in the end, I find wisdom, not in yoga, Christianity, Deepak, philosophy, or any other holy fool, but in love.

# Part IV

# Daffy and the Ducks

# ❧ 19 ❧

# One Without Wings

(DANTE, PURGATORIO, CANTO 3)

As I resume teaching in the third week of January 1999, difficulties arise. Big Daddy himself decides to take control of my mangled arm. I am such a problem that the majority of nurses refuse to touch me. "How's it feel to have so many women spurn you?" Vicki asks.

Big Daddy hazards some humor as he prepares to insert the needles. He will try the "button-hole" method—every treatment he'll stick the needles into the identical wounds, the button-holes, which will create scar tissue walls in the artery, thus making it easier to stick.

"This is an experiment?" I'm trying to force the reluctance from my voice.

"We don't use that word in the dialysis clinic," he says.

"Experiment?"

"Yes."

I'll now use the word as much possible: experiment, experimental medicine, experimental science, rat experiment.

I ask them to take me from the waiting room with the four-hour people, since I'm scheduled to teach an hour after treatment, at noon (treatment can go as late as eleven).

My Fall sabbatical has ended. Now we'll discover whether I can endure dialysis and make sense in the classroom—another experiment. No one else on the morning shift holds a job, although college teaching is hardly a job. Marginally healthy, marginally employed.

Big Daddy said they'd be happy to comply. The doctors, too, encourage patients to live as normal a life as possible. They are all willing to work with me, they say.

Yet, their timing is very erratic. Sometimes I go in early with the four-hour people; other times I find myself late and rushed to class.

Three-and-a-half hours of dialysis and it's down the highway at seventy miles an hour, driving to a small liberal arts college, which, for the purposes of this memoir, I'll call Cucumber College. Once, during sexual awareness week, the Student Life Office decided that female students required instruction in the fine art of "condom mechanics." Cucumbers were the instruments of choice. A reporter from the local newspaper got beautiful shots of happy college females and their cucumbers. Naturally, many parents and alumni were not amused. I laughed and suggested that this subject—cucumber mechanics—be offered as a major.

Coming to the end of an off-ramp, I spy a homeless person holding a sign: "Broke, Hungry, God Bless." I've heard people say: "Give 'em money and they'll head to the liquor store; give 'em a job and they'll quit after a few days." But staring at him, waiting for the light to change, the needle wounds throb sharply.

I stare and feel the suffering. Responsibility, reasons, blame, or innocent chance, his or society's, none of this seems to matter at the moment. I feel the pain in my arm.

Then a memory surfaces, something I've read or heard: Every time, a poet said, that I see a bum under an overpass I wonder if maybe this isn't a zaddik or a bodhisattva—it is a ritual with me.

Before I accelerate through the intersection, I reach out and hand him a crumpled dollar bill. On dialysis days, this becomes my new ritual. Sometimes it's a five, a ten . . .

∾

Cucumber College is the home of a well manicured, leafy campus, old brick and plaster buildings, and limited parking. Arriving near eleven, I walk half a mile. I find myself exhausted at the end of a day of walking and teaching. Yet, that afternoon, I drag myself out for a run, obstinately committed to a little denial. There are some deer in the fields, beside the road. Seeing me, they break into a headlong dash. I accelerate, trying to stay abreast of them. In a few seconds, perhaps enough to take in the humor of the situation, the deer vanish with a burst of speed, and I'm left behind, wheezing and gasping, exposed to a sharp winter wind. Run like a deer . . .

Now explain to me, beloved ministers and priests, how does such a sickly biped, hardly equipped to elude a hundred malevolent hedgehogs, how does such a joke of a species with bad teeth, weak muscles, *failed kidneys*, and a hundred other ills, the only species on the planet that runs marathons; how is this biped the paragon of nature? Can randomness contain the humor of such a claim? Or is the humor—I'm laughing between gasps of breath—a sign that randomness is present?

Yet here I am, alive and chasing wild deer, partly a creature of nature, partly a creature of economics and a technology that works most of the time. Here I stand, a primate who by accident developed a mutant brain, built a culture—an economy—and created the science that makes dialysis, as well as organ transplants, possible.

And I'm waiting for another poor bastard to die.

~

"How's school?" Big Daddy asks as he stabs the fistula.

"Through my first week," I whine. "I think I'll manage."

"Students know 'bout your illness?"

"No. Made it a point not to tell anyone. Students, colleagues . . . only a few friends. And I'm sorry I told them."

"You actually have friends in higher education?" Clinic humor.

"Don't really know. But I doubt it."

"Just as popular as with the nurses, hey?"

"Yeah, the ducks can't stand me. I'm inappropriate."

"Ducks?"

"The faculty. One just like the next, bobbing up and down on the surface of the lake, not very bright. You know, E. M. Cioran said he met philosophers living on the streets of Madrid who were more profound than any Heidelberg professor. Nietzsche's little aphorism in *Zarathustra* when he's talking about scholars: 'Like those who stand in the street and gape at the people who pass by, they too wait and gape at thoughts that others have thought.'"

Big Daddy gives a hearty laugh. "Tony, you're finally learning clinic humor."

"Sure. I'm a duck, not too bright. And I'm a duck without wings. Takes time."

"Well, you're learnin'. There's hope for you yet."

Later, driving into Cucumber College, I ask myself a question that haunted me even when healthy (at least by the numbers): How did I become one of *them*? How did it happen?

~

The buddhas in their wisdom are fairly satiated with the Billy soap opera, which has pushed all else on TV to the margins. They agree that the regular shows are more entertaining and creative. The boredom brought on by the President's stupidity has forced the buddhas to seek their distractions elsewhere. And this results in a din of constant chatter, which makes it difficult to prepare for class while on the machine.

It is Monday and Mondays are generally difficult because of the weekend weight gains. Sitting next to me, Jake crashes. I myself have yet to experience a real crash. As Jake's weekend excess is filtered out by dialysis, his blood pressure drops precipitously. Too much fluid is taken off too quickly. His blood pressure abruptly bottoms out to around 90/60. The rule is: When the blood pressure drops to these levels the patient crashes.

The first sign is cramping, then nausea, then an elevated heart rate, a cold sweat, and confusion. The first inclination is to jump up and pull out the needles. Retching generally follows, sometimes unconsciousness. Heart attack or stroke is possible.

Jake crashes and they place a plastic trough under his chin. Madonna rushes to shut off the machine's ultra-filtration, which takes off the fluid, and then pumps saline into poor Jake to increase blood volume and pressure. After a few tense minutes Jake is back, revived, but exhausted. The crash was a mild one.

I come through treatment without problems, except a miserable headache (again!), which only gets worse as I drive to Cucumber College. A cup of green tea (a craving that developed with the rise of toxins—I even chew the stuff), and I'm in the classroom talking about the French Enlightenment. Twice during the lecture, I grab the lectern to steady myself (it is my habit to walk about the room while talking). I've learned to work my dizziness into the lectures, play-acting the scenes: "And so he died . . . and so the Empire collapsed . . . and thus the Bastille fell . . ."

Lecturing, arguing with students (gently baiting them), I can feel the pain in my arm. In the sanctuary of my office, I peek under the sleeve and see that the bandages are red. My fear is that one day, waving my arms in class, the wounds will pop and blood will fly across the room. This would be far too much realism even for the fall of the Bastille. An old lady in the clinic told me that such a thing happened to her while out shopping.

I tape the bandages down. They hold. So, too, the nauseating headache.

The students never catch on. It's cool when the professor falls flat on his face.

# Deepest Dark

(DANTE, PURGATORIO, CANTO 16)

On Friday, a patient named Larry reappears after a month's absence. He sits in his usual chair, *minus his left foot*! Diabetes took his kidneys, now his foot.

His entire four hours on the machine is spent vomiting. Nothing the nurses do for him—turning the machine off, pumping in the saline, elevating his feet—cures the nausea. The charge nurse, the corpsman, tells me Larry seems beyond help.

I get off the machine quite shaken despite the fact that today I ran without problems. A kind of empathy builds in the clinic, maybe similar to the camaraderie of the trenches in the First World War. My own military experience lacked such a feeling—we were all draftees during the Vietnam War and felt nothing but abandonment. But now we're all in Larry's chair.

～

I'm leading a seminar on the German philosopher Friedrich Nietzsche. This afternoon a student, who until this moment (four weeks into the semester) had kept silent, suddenly speaks out. We're now into the later 1870s.

Nietzsche has done his essays on history, Wagner, Strauss, and Schopenhauer. I'm filling in with the nineteenth century's higher criticism of the gospels, going from Strauss to Feuerbach, Marx, Bauer.

Then I switch to Darwin.

It's all too much. She protests loudly, convinced that she needs to defend Christianity. I'm surprised since last year she took the historical Jesus course and never raised her hand. Now I hear anger, frustration, fear. "God is love!" she says.

I'm very calm, listening closely, not responding. In healthier times I might have reacted with humor, irony, and not a little sarcasm. Now I hear other things beneath her words: Fear of randomness, contingency, emptiness—a universe insensitive to her wishes—any explanation is better than none, at any cost.

Finally—still feeling my responsibility—I point out the passages to her. I patiently explain Kant's epistemology and then quote Nietzsche: "Could you think a god? Think what is thinkable . . ."

And I hear myself telling her: "But don't accept anything I say, and don't create totems."

"But the scripture says he died for our sins. Jesus says—"

"What? Even if every word in the gospels is exactly as he spoke, I would say he died too soon. All decent philosophers change their opinions in time. Look at Wittgenstein. Perhaps he might have eventually come to the conclusion that he had no need to die for us? Maybe he would have realized that he was doing us no favors. My little *sins* are my own to struggle with or enjoy, and furthermore, struggling with my sins does me good.

"Nietzsche said that when one takes away the hump from the hunchback one takes away his spirit. We might need our sins and our devils."

And maybe you need to have failed kidneys, Tony, I say to myself, as I feel the pain in my arm. And I need to answer that dilemma alone, in silence. Harvey Cox talked about visiting a Zen house in Cambridge and enjoyed it immensely because the monks left him alone. That may be a quality in religion to be coveted.

"Jesus is the same, today." She spins around and walks out of the seminar room.

~

Today they run me at a higher blood flow, four hundred and fifty milligrams a minute. Big Daddy does the needles, using the buttonhole method. I'm becoming skeptical about buttonholes; my arm constantly hurts and the wounds seem inflamed.

Off the machine and another sick headache—it's been like this all week. In the middle of my lecture an hour later, talking about the French Revolution, I suddenly feel dizzy and need to grasp the lectern to steady myself. It is a frightening moment. I thought I was about to have a seizure. In seconds, my shirt is soaked with sweat. I remember joking about "breaking a sweat" in class. I work the near collapse into the lecture . . . the death of Marat. The students never caught on. I hope.

Staggering back to my office, I started laughing. Nineteenth century Protestant theologians, mostly German, were rationalists and did not want to base their faith on miracles that violated the laws of physics. Thus, they developed the "swoon theory" to explain Christ's resurrection. Yeshua "swooned" while on the cross—went into a coma—and came out of it three days later. (Somewhat like D. H. Lawrence's story: "The Man Who Died." Unfortunately, in Lawrence's story, a certain part of his anatomy had risen with him. Lucky for him a willing priestess was near.) Well, it wasn't the Hebrew. I swooned! My office is the tomb. I simply pass out at my desk and barely make it to my next class.

Crucified in the clinic, swooning in class, emerging from the office-tomb—dialysis could cause one to develop a Christ-complex!

~

It's Monday and my fluid weight is unusually high at four kilograms, which reflects drinking too much fluid over the weekend. The nurse, Susan, sets the machine to take off the weight.

Everything goes well until 9:30 a.m., about a half hour left to go. Blood pressure is monitored every half hour; at 9:30 mine is 100/70. Ten minutes later, the words on the page begin to dance and fade. Suddenly, I experience an overwhelming nausea, dizziness, elevated heart-rate, sweating, and feelings of sinking, confusion, and terror.

And now, my death?

"I'm . . . not feeling . . . well." Somehow, I say the words but can't tell if I've given them enough volume. Susan is talking to Madonna about recipes.

Apparently, she heard. She's beside me—I think—asking something. Then she shuts off the machine and takes my blood pressure. It's 60/30, so dangerously low that my heart could slip into arrest. By now, I'm in shock. However, I hear a new noise that sounds like the roar of the ocean but must be my heart thumping its final beats. Susan calls for the charge nurse. Suddenly there's a flurry of activity about my chair. They pump in the saline and keep taking my blood pressure.

This is far worse than any swoon. Susan tilts my chair to the prone position to get blood to my brain. Then comes a dizzying darkness, a plunge into an abyss of pure nothingness. There is a frightening moment when the poor brain, still conscious, registers the fact that the organism is dying, that death is moments away. There seems to be a force pulling me down, and the strength to resist is gone. And I welcome the blanket of unconsciousness.

Slowly they bring me back. After an entire liter of saline is fed into the lines, my blood pressure rises to 90/60, still dangerously low but enough to keep my heart beating. The nurses fear that with such low blood pressure my fistula will clot. They keep checking the machine's gauges. At last, my pressure nears 100 and reality clicks back into place. My first conscious thought is the time: Is it ten yet? It is. The crash lasted for a half-hour, the fastest final half-hour I've ever experienced on dialysis. Crashes certainly make the time go.

"It's the machine," says the charge nurse, my trusted navy corpsman. "The machine zapped you. We couldn't tell it was dropping your weight so low."

"Death by machine, huh?"

"Yeah. The machine. Not our fault."

A hour later in class, my legs feel weak, hardly able to support my weight. Dizzy and nauseated, today I'm talking about Napoleon.

Napoleon possessed the ability to work for as long as twenty hours without sleep, and yet he never lost his concentration.

In the middle of discussing his Egyptian campaign, I suddenly wonder about *his* kidneys. The thought just pops into my mind. Instantly I feel ashamed. How silly to think such a thing!

Envy, anger, self-pity, egotism . . . poor little ego tossed about in an uncaring sea of randomness by the equally uncaring forces of its own DNA . . . such are the temple stones of this thought. I might have looked at anyone and asked that question, feeling so sorry for myself and so envious of the healthy.

The Buddha must have known how easy it is to slip back into the sticky ooze of selfhood, how slippery the mind can be. Low blood pressure, nausea, and, wham, self-pity!

In the Nietzsche seminar we're now reading *Also sprach Zarathustra* (in English), and I find myself talking about Darwin.

What an outcry from the students! Nothing gets them like Darwin, especially after they grasp the random nature of genetic variation and what it means for the argument from design (living nature *is not designed*, hence there's no evidence for a Designer).

Some of the students are also in a philosophy of religion course taught by a Protestant minister. In that class, the teleological argument is going strong: Everything seems designed for a specific purpose. How comforting it must be to believe that things happen for a purpose even if we don't know what that purpose is. Let's call it God's mysterious ways.

Now, despite the exhaustion, teaching is once again fun. No, I tell them, descent from the ape has never been the problem with Darwin. Why insult the innocent monkeys by blaming them for *us*? The problem is that our magnificent species may well be the result of a fortuitous match of random genetic variation with external conditions. An open geological niche happened to be available, and the mechanism of natural selection ground out Homo sapiens.

And there's no reason to doubt that we too may be a transitional species (Zarathustra's tight-rope walker) on the way to something else, or extinction. Eerily I feel my dead kidneys speaking. The innocence of chance feels more comforting than God's invisible designs.

The argument continues. I let them talk now, listening carefully, trying to catch the undertones. They're struggling: tradition, family, loved ones, revered ideas grown hoary and entrenched with age, fear too, comforting memories of childhood with its coziness and safety. I understand their confusion. Only the strong can bear truth, Nietzsche said. I've been forced to live with this aphorism.

In order to make an informed decision, one would have to spend a number of years studying the accumulated evidence for natural selection, in sciences such as biology, genetics, paleontology, geology, cosmology, maybe even artificial intelligence and chaos mathematics. The television debates, court testimony, short news articles, and other popular media are, for this reason, useless and misleading. In this age of exaggeration, misinformation, and limited attention spans, Darwin always loses. Even intellectuals can sound silly when they say things like: The best probable explanation for the fine tuning of the universe (the fifteen to twenty constants in nature that seem refined down to a vast number of decimal points) is a supernatural being of such and such qualities. But supernatural beings are fill-in-the-blank premises of what one wants to believe. It is more rational (and interesting) to search for some greater natural covering theory that explains the coincidences. And there are plenty of candidates. Even if a supernatural being should suddenly show up (and fuck with the dialysis machine—my rap lyric), how could I know the bastard was supernatural?

I tell them all this, tell them to study the evidence for themselves. But you don't need to wear Darwin like a hair shirt.

A student says that in his high school creation science is taught alongside Darwin and much to Darwin's detriment.

I surprise them: "Well, it can't really hurt. Something might actually come from it."

"Creation science?" They're mystified.

"Look at this passage in *Das frohlich Wissenschaft* (*The Gay Science*). Nietzsche speculates that logic itself must have been selected, that it arose from the rather illogical practice of seeing things as identical or equal, or distinct, or simultaneous, or caused, when none of these things are true upon close inspection. But those creatures who thought deeply about things, had insight into the flow and constant change of nature, saw that similarity does not mean identity, these creatures probably perished! *Maybe we survived by making errors.* If you're in the jungle it is better to mistake a thick vine for a deadly snake. If you're wrong, no big deal. If you're right (and your blood pressure is elevated) you've saved your life. You go home, make love, and reproduce. Mistakes could save your life."

And be especially wary of talking snakes in trees.

Now they believe that I'm contradicting myself. But the toxin fog seems to have lifted and my pickled brain appears to be working. Yet, how could I ever be sure? Could these arguments arise from the toxins?

I let the discussion meander along, this way and that, jumping from subject to subject, without conclusion, without direction, accomplishing nothing. I limit my participation to tossing in bad jokes. Getting students to smile or laugh in the midst of their "serious" rational education (add dismal too), seems to me far more valuable than meeting any course requirements. Naturally, the ducks despise such inappropriate behavior.

Plenty of hair shirts to go around.

# ᴇ 21 ᴇ

# Faith's Mysteries

(Dante, Purgatorio, Canto 18)

It is the end of February, midwinter, and I'm experiencing terrible mood swings, like the weather. One day is sunny and spring-like; the next gray and bitter cold with snow in the air. Paranoia is also a problem—I'm certain Armine is seeing another man. How could I blame her? Meditation doesn't seem to cure my dark mood. Perhaps it's the violent fluid shifts, perhaps the high level of toxins. The physicians speak mainly in terms of statistics: A certain percentage of dialysis patients suffer incurable depression—"kidney personalities."

I'm beginning to learn something about the medical profession: The best doctors are those who are able to think beyond statistics. They work from a statistical foundation, and rightly so. Nonetheless, each patient departs from these statistical truths, some by merely a tiny crack, others a yawning chasm. A good physician is able to sense these differences. A healer is able to use the technology, the science. Yet, a healer also knows when to ignore it. Medicine is in this way as much an art as a science.

One must know when to look away from statistical reality, and, especially in my case, when to pay attention.

The same holds for Deepak. The yoga sutras were my teachers. But they are far too general, too abstract. I required a guru, my own teacher, someone to adjust the practices to my own individual nature. The sutras are statistical generalizations. Once more, illness came to my rescue. Adjusting to the demands of treatment and its physical and mental limitations, along with the marginality of existence and interdependence of life, I learned from my personal guru disease that mindfulness unlocked the self and opened it for the first time to those around me, to the true beauty of the world, to real compassion and loving-kindness. So, I discovered my own way, my ninefold path.

I'm watching *Oprah* in clinic, for a few minutes, which is the limit of my endurance. She has one of those experts on again, except, I wonder, an expert in what? This guy claims that a person may come out of depression by looking at some object, like a photo for example, from happier times.

So all I need is to stare at a pair of old running shoes? And grow new kidneys?

Talk about idol worship!

∿

In the Upanishads, one reads: "You are the blue bird with the green eyes . . ." I especially love that line, but reading it in class brings me nothing but blank stares.

In Sanskrit, the meaning of Upanishad is "to sit at the feet." I do indeed have my own personal guru—I "sit at the feet" of that guru disease.

After the Western Civilization course comes Eastern Philosophy, back to back. I chuckle to myself, knowing how outraged serious professors from important universities would be at this kind of thing. But it's fun, keeps the mind active and challenged—a hazardous journey into strange and unknown landscapes where the footing is most precarious, like my experience on the slippery earth of Kauai. Yet, the most treacherous path is trying to share the journey with students.

What are my academic qualifications in Eastern Philosophy? On paper, none. But I've lived the philosophy, met the monks, learned the languages, and studied the sources obsessively. I've gone to lectures and retreats, mostly just arguing and making people miserable (kidney personality). Like many things in my life, I mastered the ideas, got bored, and went on to other things. In other words, half-assed. None of that matters now.

Today we argue about the concept of the self, and more significantly, its distant ancestor, the soul. Some students don't like the doctrine of "non-self" as it is taught by the Blessed One, the Buddha.

The self, so important and yet so difficult to actually define. I describe Plato's proof of the eternal soul in the *Phaedo*, emphasizing its Pythagorean foundations in the eternal truths of mathematics, specifically Greek geometry. Yet, now, still dizzy from dialysis, my arm aching dully, the ideas seem terribly flimsy, airless and pathetic. Plato's expansion of mathematical thinking is like Deepak's misuse of quantum mechanics, except I think Plato understands the math.

Again I listen to the objections, listen for the subterranean rumblings. The need for some self-sustained absolute, an unmoved mover, but one within, seems to call out from the dark places. Even the most skeptical people suffer this need.

I repeat the Buddha's analysis, but the students remain opposed. And yet, even as I'm talking, it strikes me as a mystery how my former self has slowly, imperceptibly, drained away. Remember to remember. Like my body adjusting to the mounting toxins, I seem to have slowly become someone else. I died and was reborn. This self is still strange to me. Hence, the changing names: Vlad, Daffy . . .

After class, a student follows me back to my office, protesting all the way. Upon graduation, she will travel to mainland China (the People's Republic) to do missionary work. She was disturbed by a statistic I quoted in class: In something like five hundred years of missionary work to the Far East, the success rate of Christianity is so tiny as to be infinitesimal. The statistic, from a history of Chinese Buddhism, goes back to the first Jesuits; communist repression cannot be blamed. Apparently, Christianity has little to commend it to that ancient culture.

I then remarked, tongue-in-cheek, that this fact was yet another objection to that argument claiming that Jesus was unique because "Look how many people follow him! If so many people believe in him then there must be something to it." One might say the same for Hitler. People willingly died for dictators too.

Again, I listen patiently. But it is tiring. Her arguments are basically negative: It could have happened such and such a way. I don't have to accept the scholars who reconstruct history. Faith is not precluded by history. No one really knows.

My arm has begun to throb and I wish she'd leave. A dialysis headache is working on me too.

Finally, between breaths, I sneak in a theological question: "Isn't it true that one who has been introduced to the Crucified and yet in the end rejects the Hebrew's divinity would be consigned to the fires that burn eternally? You know, the Church Father Tertullian thought that one of the joys of the saved in heaven was gazing down upon the torments of the damned." Tertullian, I say to myself, would have loved the dialysis clinic.

"No one knows what happens after death," she answers quickly. Again the negative.

"But isn't this a part of your faith? If not, it's still necessitated by logic: If Yeshua is the *only way*, and if I reject him, I go the *other way*. As do the Jews and the Chinese. And by the way, if no one knows, how do *you* know no one knows? Why should I believe you?"

"God can do anything."

"No doubt," I think of a number of paradoxes, "but that's beside the point." I decide on another tack. "Is God compassionate? Is Jesus?"

"Of course."

"Well, the Buddha or any bodhisattva worth his salt would insist upon sharing the fires of hell and suffering with even one single condemned soul no matter how wicked that poor soul. Which makes Buddha more compassionate."

"All other religions are frauds inspired by Satan!"

Poor Buddha! And poor professor. I keep a file of the various titles of evil I've been awarded over the years. It has grown quite fat. I'm the original Dr. Evil, by the way.

Ah, the handy scapegoat, the poor man's all-weather shelter. But I'm so tired, and feeling worse by the minute. Therefore, I shrug and say: "And we've hardly touched the historical problems. But Satan must inspire historians too!"

Then I wish her good luck in China. "Be honest, with them and with yourself."

～

Today, a bright and sunny Thursday between treatments, I'm feeling almost healthy again. In the Nietzsche seminar we're deep into *Zarathustra*, the section called "The Afterworldly." The afterwordly, says Zarathustra, construct their worlds from the very soil and grass of this one, yet they never give this world's soil the respect due to it.

And all afterworlds remain only a partial construction; they lack the pain and suffering of this world. Yet, one must also respect the negative. We need our burdens, our obstacles. We need them for their pressure. Again, I quote from Nietzsche: "Take away the hump from the hunchback and you take away his spirit. Be careful casting out demons, you may need them." We don't want others to take away our sins; we need to do the work ourselves, work though them, build on them, bridge them like a raging flood.

Verbalizing these things, and listening, I feel at peace. The afternoon's run is beneath sunny skies, breathing crisp, clean air, feeling the pain, and the pain is soothing.

# ∾ 22 ∾

# What Heavy Mood

(Dante, Purgatorio, Canto 19)

At last I am forced to bid farewell to beloved Gibbon. Coming to chapter seventy-one, I read his account of the Roman ruins. Gibbon writes: "The place and the object gave ample scope for moralizing on the vicissitudes of fortune, which spares neither man nor the proudest of his works, which buries empires and cities in a common grave." Gibbon my dear companion, you have been here in this clinic these many months, fortifying me with the long perspective, with wisdom and good humor before the melancholy vicissitudes of my own private fate.

My dialysis book for the spring will be Ron Rosenbaum's *Explaining Hitler*; next will come Kershaw's first volume of der Fuhrer's life. Suddenly at the close of the millennium, there appears to be a renewed interest in the archetype of evil, and rightly so, considering this century's blood baths.

Rosenbaum alerts me to a vast amount of work on the problem of evil, both psychological and theological, none of which I know. Oh, this cursed ignorance! Yet, I'd guess that the very quantity of such writing, like that on the historical Jesus, indicates that evil remains an intractable problem. I'm thinking about the "evil" of my kidney failure, "natural evil" as the theologians would call it—the innocence of chance according to my way of thinking.

How weak our categories for explaining evil. The Polish poet Alexander Wat said that this century gives little proof of the existence of God; Satan, however, is irrefutably present.

On the very day I begin Rosenbaum, a student from the Eastern Philosophy class tells me that her eighty-four-year-old grandfather shot himself to death over the weekend. Tears fill her eyes as she speaks.

I cannot think of anything to say, anything even half way meaningful. The old man wasn't sick, gave no signs, displayed no mental disturbances. It seems he simply decided that it was time to go.

Naturally, my own brush—continuing brush—with the Dark One comes to mind, how I began to slowly fade and disengage, how death didn't appear so terrible as life slowly drained away. Suddenly I can imagine the old man as he experienced the evaporation of his powers, and how one day he finally decided that enough was enough, with no regrets.

That afternoon out running (dragging myself is more accurate), a thought comes: Perhaps awareness is a curse? The tragedy of cognition, the philosophers say. *We know* (or, at least some one does know, but I have yet to meet this fortunate fellow or lady).

Maybe the old Gnostics had it right: We are the bungled creation of a rather deluded, jealous god who, like a watchmaker wearing thick, fingerless mittens, assembled us from plans he-she-it could barely decipher. The thought causes me to laugh. Good god, what would the therapists say if they heard that one?

It is late March, a beautifully warm and bright day. I'm running a nature trial and the wild vegetation is beginning to awaken from its winter death, and the flora gives off aromatic perfume, which is the true odor of resurrection. And yet, the depressing thought persists.

Was self-aware consciousness selected, contributing to the survival of our species? But like all developments, there must be some trade-off, call it an entropy factor, a negative balancing the positive. Consciousness permits us to agonize over such questions, the Kantian "aspiration" of reason to strive for such absolutes. Yet, this aspiration does not mean that such goals are attainable or even thinkable. It is a design flaw, one might say, like my damned kidneys. I have to laugh at my own gullibility, at the ideas I willingly swallowed. Daffy indeed. Look at the silliness I bought in the desperation of gazing into the black tunnel. Once I gave up belief things improved.

With the approach of death, I remember feeling less anxious, less fearful, more and more disengaged (that word again!); even the question of my illness appeared laughable, that is, ridiculous and insulting that I should ponder the riddle.

So why did the old man kill himself? A koan.

~

Today I come off dialysis with another sick headache. My blood pressure is inching up again. The doctors don't know why. My wife shakes her head and says it's the disease—hypertension.

Dr. Jung doubles the blood pressure medicine. This tends to slap me down, to drain away what energy remains.

I've begun keeping a blood pressure log. There appears to be a pattern: several weeks of low pressures, including a number of crashes, followed by weeks of high pressures—up and down. The high pressures bring black clouds of irritability and frightful storms of thundering rage. It seems that the personality changes are like early spring weather. I suddenly become a person I absolutely loathe. Could this be an example of the self's fluidity?

Richard Dawkins claims that genes exert a statistical influence upon human behavior, and yet this influence can be modified, over-ridden or reversed by other influences (*The Selfish Gene*).

It's meditation versus high blood pressure. So far, no contest.

How has kidney failure changed my personality and thinking? Certainly in profound ways of which I'm hardly aware, perhaps will never be aware. I've tried to record the more obvious ways; yet, how complex is human behavior! And yet again, do our vaunted higher mental functions, of which we're so proud, exist and operate at the whim of dumb molecules?

Today, Cucumber College's resident minister stormed into my office after the Nietzsche seminar and demanded to know if I believed in sin. A student from Eastern Philosophy had been arguing with him, and it wasn't long before he guessed the source of the argument.

"No, don't believe in sin," I answered quickly, "but I do believe Origen when he wrote that 'sloth and weariness of taking trouble to preserve the good, coupled with disregard and neglect of better things, began the process of withdrawal from the good.'"

"That's not sin?"

"Origen might think so. I don't. We just get lazy."

He left shaking his head.

Next morning in clinic, I observe that Billy, now in his post-Monica funk, has ordered the bombing of Yugoslavia. We watch the smart bombs as they home in on their prey.

# ↝ 23 ↜

# Tears and Laughter

(DANTE, PURGATORIO, CANTO 21)

I'm reading John S. Feinberg's memoir on suffering, *Deceived by God.* Feinberg is a theologian, professor of theology, and the author of a scholarly work about God and evil. His wife was diagnosed with Huntington's disease, a genetic disease that is incurable and progressively debilitating.

Feinberg believes that God is active in the tiniest minutia of life. It was God's will, he writes, that he and his wife marry and have children. They'd asked God and received His assent. Although Feinberg does not reveal the particulars, it is apparent that they never would have married if God said NO. They knew nothing about her genetic condition, which could easily have been passed on to their children.

Naturally, this resonates. I can hardly glance at my children without wondering.

Feinberg, however, wants to know what on earth (or in heaven) God could have been thinking when He "ordered" them to marry? Why didn't God tell us then? Feinberg wonders.

I'm reading the book on a soccer field, waiting for my daughter's game to start, surrounded by believers like Feinberg.

Is God so evil that He delights seeing His children suffer? No, Professor Feinberg answers emphatically (obviously he rejects Schopenhauer). It is true that there is never a good time to receive such news, but God knew exactly the right time to reveal his wife's illness (is he serious?). No matter how much turmoil and pain one suffers, he goes on, one must focus on God's goodness—things could be far worse, more than one could imagine (yeah, and somewhere they *are*). And, of course, there's sin and Satan. It's amazing, muses Professor Feinberg, that anything ever goes right (it's amazing how any explanation is better than none)!

Having let God off the hook, the professor next turns his attention to what *not* to say to sufferers. The answer to suffering, he lectures, is not intellectual but emotional. He has all the intellectual answers, he brags (and I cannot say whether he does or not, having not read his big book on evil), yet he still felt betrayed. These are natural feelings and one should not try to repress them. Rather, we must focus on the fact that God still cares, still loves us, if only we'd look in the right places. After all, there's life eternal for believers (constructed from the soil and grass of this one?).

Reading this, I could laugh and cry at the same time. Chance robbed of its innocence, the inability to accept life as it is, a blindness to, indeed hatred of, reality . . . a world that is unthinkable outside language evolved in this world, which poisons, toxifies (I know something about toxins!), depreciates this world. . . . I scribble these incomplete thoughts in the margins and continue reading. The real living game has yet to begin.

He says that God uses suffering to educate others (bystanders? skeptics?). Divine lesson plans? It is as if the Divine Mind, with its Divine Imagination and Divine Creativity, could not conceive of a thousand alternative means of teaching the identical lesson, none at such lethal costs. Is God so lacking in imagination that He must resort to brutality? And what exactly is He trying to teach? That life is suffering? Turn back to the Preface of this book; the Buddha taught this, but so much more softly, quietly. God apparently feels the need of making a big noise in the world. Perhaps He suspects no one will believe in Him without Divine pyrotechnics?

No! I'm being absurd. Professor Feinberg sternly warns us that we the creature cannot judge God by our own standards. This is one I've heard before. And why not? What other standards have we? If, as Feinberg must believe (which I do not), the moral standards by which we judge good and evil must come from God, then apparently God cannot be held accountable by His own standards. This makes him a bloody-handed dictator standing above the law. Feinberg keeps making the point that we can't fully understand God's purposes or justice. If this is so, maybe God hates the dear professor and his wife? Maybe God enjoys their suffering? Maybe God desires that we hate Him, or don't believe in Him, in order to be saved (see Ockham on such ideas). And even if God lets us in on the joke (revelation), we'd only be able to grasp the riddle by our standards. We have no others.

The soccer game has started and I close the book for the time being. Thankfully the game has brought me back to the glory of a beautiful spring day and healthy children.

I'm beginning to think of Professor Feinberg as "suffering incorporated." Nearing the end of the memoir, Professor Feinberg is getting preachy and boring. Actually, he seems rather cold-hearted, more concerned with his own reactions to his wife's suffering. It is so damned difficult not to become a prisoner of one's personal pain.

At the conclusion of the book, Professor Feinberg's wife is graciously given a few pages of her own. Naturally, she blesses the Holy One, and hopes that her suffering brings faith to many people. Apropos to this hope, she adds—without the slightest irony (or good taste)—that her disease gave her and her husband the opportunity to witness Christ to her Jewish neurologist!

~

Today, the Monday after Easter, they couldn't stop the bleeding once the needles had been removed. Synchronicity? After fifteen minutes of holding the gauze, I still spurted blood. Yet, my blood pressure is low.

They also seem to be having more trouble with my fistula. Even Big Daddy had problems with me this morning. And the blood flow has fallen to four hundred. No one knows why. Big Daddy says that the fistula ought to be maturing, getting larger and thicker. In fact, it's shrinking. I'm getting into the habit of crashing Mondays: My blood pressure drops to ninety, then the eighties. I break out into a sweat, the room begins to spin, and then I pass out.

Teaching after a crash becomes surreal. I stagger into class, dizzy, sick, hardly able to focus, simply trying to get through the hour. The students say that I'm relaxed, laid-back. I have to rely upon my memory for the lecture, which is becoming more and more like a torn net—the facts keep slipping out, and I vainly try to capture them like so many squirming fish.

Professor Feinberg gave a little lecture at the close of his book on the ease of building an *incorrect* case about God through "inferential reasoning." Before we accuse God of anything, we need to look closely at the evidence and make certain we interpreted it *correctly*. Looking long and hard enough, Feinberg is confident we'll see the truth that God is innocent.

Ah, dear Professor, *how* do I distinguish between correct and incorrect inferences? What about the flow of this or that fluid, according to the mad marquis? How tight are the bonds of chemistry on my mind? Can I trust my reasoning? And don't tell me Scripture! Scripture speaks with a chorus of voices; God has a thousand faces. I can find *anything* I wish in Scripture, from sublime compassion to the most bestial cruelty.

I prefer the rabbis in the concentration camps who put God on trial, found Him guilty, and then went for evening prayer.

Now, still feeling sick, I'm in the Eastern Philosophy class beginning the discussion of Zen. It's eerie how subjects based upon a tentative syllabus written months ago speak to my feelings and experiences on a particular day. I'm trying to explain the problem Zen was meant to solve: The desire to escape desire is itself a desire and hence an attachment (is this your desire for God, dear Professor Feinberg? Maybe you were truly deceived?). The desire to achieve enlightenment is an attachment, I tell them, and here we have the age-old problem of foundations.

The students are enthralled with Zen. Perhaps it's Zen's exotic nature, its general rebelliousness. Perhaps it's Zen's rejection of abstractions and insistence upon simplicity, seeing directly into things. But doing so is not easy. In a Zen monastery, one is put to work. The student never knows when the instruction will begin, just plant, sweep, take out the garbage, clean the latrines . . . and shut your mouth. I wonder if Yoga Madonna submits to such discipline?

~

It is late April and the night of the Student Awards Ceremony. We professors march into the auditorium adorned in academic robes.

I forgot my robes. The toxins erode short-term memory. But no one believes that I've forgotten my garb. Everyone thinks it is an act of rebellion as befitting my reputation at Cucumber College. Inferential reasoning, Professor Feinberg!

I didn't protest this inference. I could have pulled back my sleeve and showed them the stigmata. But I didn't say a word.

I merely smiled.

The blood flow is still dropping. My fistula goes into spasms at least once every treatment. The red light blinks. The infernal high-pitched buzzer sounds.

Rosenbaum talks about the power of suggestion. Hitler told all his cronies that his beloved niece Geli was blonde and very tall, regal and beautiful, and all of them remembered her as such. Yet, actual photographs show her with dark hair, rather common looks, and of average height.

Inferential reasoning and the power of suggestion; how difficult it is to see clearly.

# Part V

# Neo Tubes

# ～ 24 ～

# Will Divine

(Dante, Purgatorio, Canto 21)

Crashes on the dialysis machine are like dropping through the floor. I'm reading while the blood flows out, through the tubes, and back into my arm. Suddenly an invisible door beneath me opens and I drop through, and keep falling into darkness.

During my last crash, I dreamed of a little devil standing next to the trapdoor, holding a lever, and closing it behind me. Maybe he's Maxwell's demon. The nineteenth century physicist James Clerk Maxwell imagined a little demon in order to illustrate entropy: His demon, possessing superhuman reflexes, opens and closes the door of a pressurized cylinder allowing only the most energetic molecules to exit—entropy. But if the demon allowed only the lesser energetic molecules to exit, this would be entropy reversal, forbidden by thermodynamics.

I name my devil Maxwell. His swinging trapdoor leads out of this world.

I crash and drop out of the world. Maxwell shuts the door and for the moment, I hang suspended and engage in a chat with the little fellow.

Sometimes it's very difficult grasping what he says. His sentences are broken. He speaks with a slight accent, one I cannot identify; perhaps, at times he sounds German or Eastern European. He appears to be an affable little guy, neatly dressed in lime trousers and yellow golf shirt. He looks as if he's just off the course and headed for the clubhouse. But he stops to open that damned door and then lingers to have a word with me.

"It's so easy to drop right through the floorboards. Ja?"

Groggy, light-headed, floating, blood pressure nearing 80/50, it's hard to focus. The nurses are hovering, taking my pressure, giving me saline.

"The floor . . . the walls too, the ceiling . . . just drop away."

"There. I'll close the door."

"Am I lost?"

"Ever lose a sock?"

"Oh yeah."

"That's me. Open the trapdoor."

"You . . . you look like you've just come off the eighteenth hole."

"Ja, ja. Been playing a round with your buddy Feinberg."

"You? A devil? Didn't he whack you instead of the ball?"

Maxwell gives a gentle chuckle. "Oh no. He didn't even recognize me, by God!"

"He didn't?"

"Nope. He even told me 'bout his wife. She's quite ill, not so? Worse than you, I'd wager."

"Yeah. And?"

"He thinks that there's some purpose behind it all, that God's up there." Maxwell points a manicured finger at the door, which I suddenly notice is painted bright red, like my tubes. "That God orders things up there like some movie director—call Him, say, Will Divine."

"Who doesn't seem very creative these days," I interrupt him.

"They don't like taking risks. But Feinberg thinks God's a super director behind every drifting dust-mote, even the roll of his ball on the green. So there must be a reason why good ole God didn't tell him about his wife's illness."

"So what has this got to do with movie directors?"

Maxwell, whose features are beginning to come into focus—he looks very distinguished, goatee, white hair, fine-lined dark skin—suddenly appears disappointed.

"Stupid! Thought you were brighter than that!"

"Sorry. Beaner's pickled."

"Must be. Don't you see that people like Feinberg are the first to join up?"

"Join up?"

"Join up, join in, enlist! The party, the movement, the church, anything with a director. Think about the world up there."

"The clinic?"

Maxwell gives a soft laugh. "Clinic is a good word for it. Its Feinbergs are the unwitting guards, prepared to do anything, think anything, in order to prove their point: If God rules the world, there must exist at least a little residue of organization hanging around, and all events, no matter how terrible, must have some divinely inspired meaning. It's usually embodied in the Party, the Book, the Church—the Director."

"Aren't you exaggerating?"

"Am I? On the golf course just now, Feinberg told me a story. A couple lost their daughter to an auto accident.

Yet, these parents claimed that people came to know the Lord through this dreadful event, and became good church members. And thus they concluded that the death of their daughter was for the best."

"Preposterous! There's something . . . evil about that kind of thinking!"

"Evil?" Maxwell inclines his head. "Up there, past that door, such an explanation is called good."

"The clinic—"

"Ja, think about it: If they can say such things about their own daughter, then imagine how easy it is accepting the deaths of other's children in the name of the Lord. Millions upon millions."

"Makes your job easier, hey my little friend?"

"How else do you think I can take so much time off to play golf?"

Saturday, April 17, at five in the morning, my phone rings. The call took me completely by surprise, as would any call at five on a Saturday morning. It was the transplant coordinator, a nurse I have known for about a year. She squeaks when she talks, thinks I'm about age five, and is working on her doctorate in nursing. She calls herself PhDc – the "c" for candidate. I name her Sutra Cindi because she makes such an effort to be soothing, which for kidney personalities can be sickening.

"We have a kidney for you, Anthony, from someone your age." Instantly I realize someone has just died, someone like me with a family, loved ones who at this moment are devastated. Now I do feel sick. I wish Maxwell would lock that door!

"The antigen match is three out of six," she says.

Antigens are chromosomal markers indicating tissue types; a good match lowers, according to many physicians, the rejection factor.

Three out of six? A fifty percent match? Would I bet on such a horse?

I hesitate. "Why don't you call the surgeon?" she suggests.

I do. But he's not *my surgeon*. I've never met him. He sounds sleepy, uninvolved. Oh, it's a good match, he mumbles without excitement or conviction. I forget that for him kidney transplant surgery is like changing a tire.

I sit up in the bed and think. The antirejection drugs will destroy my immune system. I've only three weeks to go in the semester. If I exercise some patience, I might get a better match, say a five or a six (later I discover that no one gets such matches).

How easy it is to rationalize.

Actually, I'm scared, sweating and trembling. I picture the knife cutting into my abdomen (where they put the new kidney), burning like fire. I feel the searing, picture the blood, think about the soft bandage, the stitches, and long recovery.

I call Sutra Cindi and decline the kidney. She doesn't argue.

I tell myself I made the right decision. I *felt* that this wasn't the time, that it wasn't *the kidney*. Follow your gut feelings . . .

The reason I refused was far more banal and less rational: I was scared!

"So now you understand most people," Maxwell says to me as he holds the trapdoor lever. "Aren't most decisions made in such a manner? Feelings. Trust or don't trust. If they're agreeable they come from God. If disturbing, they come from devils like myself. What's dangerous is to have such feelings covered all over with good intentions, and then begin to have them take over."

"Couldn't pump up my courage."

"Didn't Nietzsche call it proof by potency? If it feels good, it must be true? Many believers think this way. You did too. Remember when you were Daffy? Perhaps such feelings, divine or demonic, are there to lead us to ruin and should be resisted rather than followed."

"You devils argue so well," I sigh.

"Ah, Tony, I'm not finished. How different are you from them? Weren't you driven by fear? Didn't you rationalize? Tell yourself likely stories? And the more you contemplated your stories, chewing them like a cow, the better you felt about a decision driven by blind fear. So now do you understand why they cling to their faith like a miserable piece of wreckage tossed about by those Heraclitean storms?"

"Damned devil!"

Maxwell laughs softly.

Soberly considered, however, the transplant answer to kidney failure seems gruesomely barbaric. It's like cut and paste historical writing: taking your sources and quoting them whole, like islands, with sentences of your own here and there that serve to create currents between the dense rocks of block quotes. It's amateurish. It's boring. Cut and paste history is usually found in freshman or sophomore papers. It happens when the student is rushed or just plain lazy.

Transplant is the cut and paste of medicine, cut the organ out of the corpse, sew it into the living person like a block quote. There's a scene from a Star Trek movie, *Star Trek IV*, in which the crew returns to twentieth century San Francisco in search of a whale. They find themselves in a hospital. A moaning woman, obviously in pain, catches Dr. McCoy's attention. What's wrong? he asks. Dialysis, she whines. Dialysis! exclaims an indignant

Bones, is this the Middle Ages? He gives her a pill. Later, she cries out happily: "I grew a new kidney!"

Science usually catches up with science fiction, sometimes surpassing it. With stem cell research, cloning, and nanotechnology (the engineering of matter on the molecular, maybe even atomic level), such a scene may someday play out in real life. Growing kidneys and other organs will replace transplant. Dr. Jung, however, warned me that this is probably fifty years or more away. Until then, there is only cut and paste.

∾

Now in April, my fistula slowly begins to fail. Little by little, the blood flow decreases: From four hundred and fifty it drops to four hundred, then three-fifty. The machine is the same. Big Daddy continues to stick the buttonholes. There's no deviation from my routine. The stability of the routine creates an illusion of security.

There should be no more problems until transplant, says Dr. Jung.

And the little devil Maxwell softly laughs as he opens the door beneath my feet.

# ⤝ 25 ⤜

# Profoundest Night

(Dante, Purgatorio, Canto 23)

Monday. Three hours into treatment, my blood pressure suddenly drops to 80/50. My heart begins to race. I'm drenched in cold sweat, and the room begins to spin. A crash. But this time Maxwell opened the door without a word.

Vicki takes my pressure and then shuts down the ultra-filtration. She opens the saline clamp. Then she takes another pressure.

"I can't get a reading," she says. She calls to the navy corpsman, the charge nurse. The verdict is more saline.

The corpsman shakes his head: "We'll have to raise his target weight" (this means that they're taking off too much fluid, making me too dry).

"Raise target weight." Things are quite automatic in clinic. Even semiconscious, I predicted that he'd say this.

Slowly I climb out of the black hole. It takes a half-hour, the duration of today's treatment. Today, the third Monday in April, is a fifteen-minute day. Having finished our blood-letting, we must sit with the arterial needle still inserted for a period of fifteen minutes, after which they take a syringe of blood to measure the effectiveness of dialysis, the ratio KT/V.

I stagger out of the clinic into a warm April sun. My arm hurts like the devil, but my headache is worse.

It's a miracle I'm able to walk about. Somehow, I manage to teach my two classes, making jokes and telling stories. No one knows.

Back in my office, sipping green tea, the future missionary to the heathen Chinese walks in. She feels a need to argue, to defend Christianity against me. Wearily I tell her that I'm not attacking her religion. Maxwell's words are still in my mind.

But she says that she really wants to hear the arguments against it.

I sigh and ask: "Well, do you really believe that two individuals, Adam and Eve, by their free acts of will brought death into the world?"

We've been talking about original sin these days.

We go round and round about "spiritual death," and "star death," and Darwin. *I* feel like death.

All the time, like a subliminal voice, my arm throbs with a dull pain. This is odd. Usually the pain from the needles goes away in an hour or two. Today it actually seems to increase. Yet, I pay little attention to it.

"Death was here long before we popped in to pollute the place," I tell her, thinking about my own kidney failure. Am I responsible? Did anyone ask me to choose my genes before birth?

Maybe illness has made me *more* spiritual. Take away the hump from the hunchback . . . Ah, but here I am asking about the man who shot me with the poisoned arrow. For anyone who seriously thinks about religion, dilemmas ultimately arise, and headaches ensue. Theology gave Darwin indigestion.

Mercifully, the missionary girl finally gives up and leaves. This event is the strongest proof yet *for* the existence of God.

About five in the afternoon, I arrive home. Sitting in my car, without conscious decision, I touch my fistula.

And feel nothing! No hum of blood. No thrill. No pulse. Only the pain. It must be a hallucination.

My wife confirms the diagnosis. Blood flow in the access has ceased.

On the phone, Dr. Jung orders me back to the clinic. It's strange in the late afternoon; most of the nurses are the same, but the patients are different.

Despite the pain, I experience a wave of sympathy. I only endure this place for three-and-a-half hours, but for the nurses it's the entire day.

The corpsman confirms what I already know: The fistula has shut down. He says that it's clotted off, a rather common event. Until this moment, I've never heard of such common events—once more, it is the medical policy of information by slow drip.

Blood clots can be cleared by the injection of a drug, a clot-buster that dissolves the clot. In reluctant cases, they insert a catheter-tipped balloon pump and mechanically stretch the artery.

Dr. Jung calls. I'm to present myself at 7:30 a.m. Tuesday at the hospital, where I'm to be admitted for the day. I'll have to cancel my classes. No, I shouldn't need to stay the night.

Hospital Administration. Maybe fainting would speed up the process. Probably not. From my experience in clinic, I know that no matter how sick a person is, there's nothing that supersedes the hospital employee's right to a break, or protocol.

It looks like I'll never get past Hospital Administration. I've forgotten my insurance card (actually I'm carrying the wrong one). It doesn't seem to matter in the least that I'm a regular customer at this hospital—since 1991!—that my insurance has always paid for everything, that I'm still working. No insurance card, no admittance!

Fortunately, my wife's HMO card gets me in. Another proof of God's existence.

I'm admitted to a double room. The other patient is an old fellow from a rural county north of here. He's in for a "heart procedure," he says. He talks to me but I can barely understand. His family comes for a visit. Every single member is overweight. Periodically one leaves for a smoke. And I'm the one in the hospital with a life-threatening illness.

Sitting on the bed, I read about the Boston Marathon in the newspaper. I suddenly recall the 1980 race when I finished and began to urinate blood. Could kidney failure have begun then?

The techs finally arrive to take me down to radiology. Again! And everything is the same. I'm strapped down, needle in the arm, that massive camera nearly crushes me to the steel table. They inject the dye that burns from neck to shoulder.

I still am unable to accustom myself to the small talk among the nurses and techs. To them the entire procedure is just a job, repeated so often that it's boring. To me it's the inquisition, torture, and execution.

The procedure lasts an hour. The radiology doctor examines the screen. "There's no clot here," he says, pointing to the dark branch-like arteries and veins. "Up near the elbow . . . it appears that your vein has narrowed and the blood flow's cut off. Could be scar tissue. Could be an anatomical fluke. But the fistula can't be salvaged."

Radiology has spoken.

I'm wheeled back to my room. The old man has vanished, along with his family.

Dr. Jung comes in along with the vascular surgeon. "You'll need a new fistula," says Dr. Jung. "The old one has closed off. It was never right from the start. It's your anatomy. Happens in two percent of the cases."

"So I'm the fortunate two percent."

They confer and decide to place a new fistula in my upper arm, in the artery along my bicep. "It'll take time to mature, naturally. About eight weeks." Later he tells me six weeks to make me feel better.

"I can't go without dialysis?"

"No. We'll have to put in a subclavial catheter. We'll run a tube underneath your clavicle and into the heart vein. The catheter is located in your chest right under the skin. Two tubes hang down, arterial and venous lines. We'll do both procedures on Wednesday. They're fairly routine."

With that, they both leave. The old man returns, drugged, with a hole in the groin. He shifts in bed and the hole bleeds. A nurse comes in and sits with him, applying pressure.

Reading has become impossible (too shaken to concentrate), so I turn on the TV and discover that while I was in radiology there was a massacre in a high school outside Denver. Two students walked into Columbine High and blasted away with an assortment of firearms (most of their homemade bombs failed to explode). They killed thirteen, and themselves. Juxtaposed with this story is the bombing of Yugoslavia. Back and forth, from massacre to massacre.

As I drift into a fitful sleep, I hear a politician blame the high school killings on violent movies and video games. A gaggle of experts agree. But how do they explain Yugoslavia?

What would Kafka or Celine make of this madhouse?

～

The techs finally come at noon. They wheel me down to Same Day Surgery. An IV is inserted into my good arm. I'm given papers to sign: "Be aware of the risks of surgery," say bold, block letters at the top of the page. I am becoming aware, yes.

In the anteroom, there's another long wait. I'm apparently in line, like an airliner waiting to take off. It's also the noon hour—lunch.

About 1 p.m., they wheel me into the operating room. Once more, I'm overwhelmed—dazzled—by the large, brilliant lights like tiny suns, the number of people milling about, the machines. I don't see the surgeon.

Now I'm on the cold steel table. Somebody is asking about the history of science, and I hear myself talking about Einstein's first relativity paper (1905), but I'm becoming groggy and probably not making any sense.

When they created my first fistula back in March of 1998, I remember seeing the vascular surgeon. He introduced a resident who would be assisting him. Not this time. The anesthesiologist cuts me off mid-sentence. A good thing.

Absolute and total darkness: no saints, no Hebrew prophets, no Vishnu, Brahma, or Shiva. No Madonna or Oprah.

Pain. Sharp, persistent pain in my upper arm, all the way to the shoulder. Armine is there, bending over me, saying something. They pump in the drugs and I slide back into a drifting, chemically cushioned cloud.

Once the pain subsides, I find myself awestruck by the nature of lived time. Armine says that the surgery took three hours; for me, it was like closing my eyes for a brief nap, surely no more than a few seconds. Is this death? A second of darkness while a whole eternity passes? In cosmology, one might say that the universe contracts into a singularity given the prerequisite dark matter, and time begins to slow, at last creeping to nothing. For the dead, it is a timeless moment: no past, no future, simply the now, the moment, an eternal moment. Maybe I'm beginning to grasp Zen.

The pain brings me back to normal consciousness. Now there's pain in my chest and neck. Suddenly I'm aware of the tubes hanging down over my right nipple. A large, square bandage covers my right breast; a smaller bandage is taped to the base of my neck. "They had to thread the catheter," Armine tells me, "that's why there's an incision in your neck."

Another dose of drugs begins to take effect, and I'm floating into a dulled, dopey state. Then they wheel me off to dialysis in the hospital. Dialysis is easy—no sticking, no needles, merely connecting the tubes to the machine. Afterward I'm wheeled back to my room. The old man and his hefty family are gone. The drugs are making me giddy, slipping in and out of consciousness.

Vaguely, I note that the television is dominated by the high school killings. Endless interviews, videotape of students fleeing the school, SWAT teams charging in, endless reporters looking concerned and dour, and very important.

At last, I drop off into a deep sleep, watching Al Gore mourn.

~

A revelation comes while listening to the therapists and pols discussing Columbine and obsessions with movie violence: *I experienced a synchronistic event!*

The Sunday before the fistula breathed its last, I went with my teenage son Luc to see the movie *The Matrix*. In one scene, the hero named Neo is rescued from the evil machines. His neck, chest, arms and torso sprout plugs and tubes, the terminals that connected him to the machines. I recall thinking at the time how grotesque they looked, how I preferred my temporary needles, how Neo was a plug-in fellow sufferer. Today I'm a real plug-in monster! Neo Tubes. In this dazed condition it's even difficult telling where fantasy ends and reality begins. Then I hear *The Matrix* blamed for the shootings.

Mercifully, the nurse enters my room and pumps in more drugs.

It takes the entire morning for the hospital bureaucracy to discharge my drugged carcass. Unable to obtain the required signatures on the required forms, it is possible that the nurses forged them to get me out of there.

Because my kidneys no longer clear fluids, the super painkillers are recycled through my system, and I sleep around the clock, spending the rest of the time in my chair drooling. The gruesome tubes sprouting from my chest work well enough in dialysis—in fact, they're a great deal easier than sticking. The nurses open the clamps at the tubing nozzles, draw out two syringes of blood, and attach the nozzles to the machine. In no time I'm off and running "like a deer." Anybody can do it. Clinic policy can now be followed to the letter.

While I was away, a new satellite clinic opened in a small town north of here, which means that my friend

Jake has departed, along with many of the other buddhas like Philip R. Mostly the old people remain, sleeping peacefully through treatment. Soon I find, surprisingly, that I miss the chatter. What comfort we take from the familiar, no matter how irritating.

It takes nearly three days for the drugs to wear off. Without drugs, there's plenty of pain in the wounds. In clinic, they change the dressings and I feel the pull of raw skin around the catheter (which I cannot see). My upper arm stings whenever I move it. The new fistula, however, is buzzing and keeps me awake at night. But so, too, did the old one.

Maxwell whispers: "Any regrets?"

"For what?"

"Turning down that kidney."

"Damned devil! Never occurred to me."

"Well?"

"I refuse to even think about it. Just makes the pain worse, like the Buddha taught. Another arrow in my flesh."

Maxwell vanishes as Dr. Jung walks into the clinic. I ask him when—and how—I can run. He looks at me as if he's prepared to commit me to the state mental hospital. He's never had anyone with a catheter ask about running. Such things do not find their way into medical texts.

"About four weeks," he finally answers. But I can see that he'd pulled the figure out of thin air.

After a week, I'm out running again.

∼

Who knows what people hide? In *The Meditations*, Descartes imagined that the people he saw walking outside his window could easily be mechanical automatons covered by clothes. That fits me! I walk into Cucumber College on Monday morning, tubes firmly taped over my right nipple—they sprout from my chest like onion shoots, like those terminals from *The Matrix*. No one knows.

Absent for a week, I'm met by a mighty wave of indifference. The students were grateful for a week off, especially at the end of the semester. My colleagues could care less; the administration would care only if they had to pay.

Classes are a struggle. My blood pressure keeps falling, leaving me weak and light-headed. I don't know if I'm even making sense. Lectures sound disjointed and hesitant, and I'm sure I'm making mistakes. Yet, a student tells me, "you're really laid back, man . . ."

The next day in the Nietzsche seminar, about an hour or so into the class, I suddenly stop. The mind, or brain, or consciousness, or whatever this strange instrument is called, simply ground to a halt. Thought abruptly ceased, like a stream suddenly going dry. A few minutes of embarrassing silence ensued, once again proving Einstein's theories on time: that time grinds to a halt in a powerful gravitational field, like a black hole. Finally, consciousness returned, the electricity came back on, and I mustered enough wit to end the class.

Back in my office, I noticed that the front of my shirt had turned red. The gauze bandage over the wound in my neck was soaked through. The incision was bleeding. Later I discovered that the clinic had increased my dose of heparin in order to keep the catheter clear of clots, which in turn caused the blood to flow more freely from my wounds.

A change of dressing and some pressure stopped the bleeding. Frightened, I thought that the end had come. Fortunately, I was too weak to slip into real panic or hysteria, merely a mild angst. Whether or not the students noticed remains unknown.

The next day in clinic the gauze is replaced by a regular drugstore Band-Aid. I must be on the road to recovery.

While I'm adjusting to the tubes, the nurses are riveted to continual replays of the Littleton tragedy. The horde of psychologists, docs, revs, priests, pols, and therapists that crowd the screen bemoan the violent culture of videos, movies, games. But there's certainly as much violence in Homer—*The Iliad* begins with the word *wrath*. As Herodotus says, Homer was the teacher of Greece. And Greece was the teacher of Western civilization. And what about Scripture? YHWH is a man of war, we're told in Exodus, and he proves it innumerable times. The holy slaughters go on—blessed of course. There seems to be no end to it, well, except the *final* end, which is a slaughter of nature.

Many people wonder if these kids showed early signs of trouble.

I'm reading Kershaw's *Hitler: Hubris*. After discussing young Adolf's troubled childhood, Kershaw still says that the seeds of der Fuhrer did not grow from that soil, that no one could have found the future dictator in the abused child. Even predictability after the event takes the sting out of uncertainty.

∽

I notice for the first time that one of the older patients has returned to clinic; he'd been missing for two weeks and I thought that he'd been assigned to another clinic. But today he's back in a wheelchair. He suffered a stroke.

Today I also learned (from the social worker) that the Medicare reimbursement for a single dialysis treatment is $129.70, thanks to the Social Security Act of 1972— and a New York City salesman named Shep Glazer who walked into the hearing of the House Ways and Means Committee, chaired by Wilbur Mills, and had himself dialyzed. The demonstration apparently convinced Congress to give financial aid to kidney patients.

Still working (although I've never thought of Cucumber College as work), my insurance pays the bills. The rate for insurance is $450.00 a treatment.

## ⤙ 26 ⤚

# Seraphim

(Dante, Purgatorio, Canto 5)

We conclude the Nietzsche seminar reading *The Antichrist*. I point out to them the familiar line: "Convictions are prisons."

After class, the soon-to-be missionary corners me. She will graduate this month. She's had the History of Christianity course and now the Nietzsche seminar. She's still a good Christian, she triumphantly announces.

I protest (weakly) that I'm not out to convert anybody to anything. If convictions are prisons, then this is true for anything I have to say. And remember what Zarathustra says: "One repays a teacher badly if one remains nothing but a pupil." So, forget me and find yourself.

"Well, I don't believe Nietzsche!" she says emphatically. "I've withstood the temptations."

"This, then, should be noted on your diploma," I say.

∼

I am trying to run with the grotesque tubes, which swing back and forth and pull at the flayed skin about the catheter. The wound has become raw. I tape the tubes down, but the sweat soaks through and the tape comes free . . . and the tubes are back to swinging with each step. As the days grow warmer, I sweat more, causing further irritation.

There are weight problems too since fluid loss during my runs skews dry-weight numbers (again!), and, god forbid, the lab nurses have to change the computer.

Yesterday Vicki put a different bandage over my tubes, one made from cloth that soaks up the moisture better than the gauze.

Meanwhile I'm grading term papers on the machine. The nurses come by, glance at the titles, and groan. "The Mahayana Concept of Emptiness According to Nagarjuna Compared to Phenomenology" will never make it on *Oprah*. Later, Vicki tells me that it's the consensus among the nurses that my classes must be incomprehensible.

~

Friday, after treatment, I turn in my grades for the semester. Afterward a student drops by and we talk, and I have the odd experience of hearing an argument I'm continually making come from the mouth of someone else. I suddenly realize how stupid the argument sounds.

Ashamed, I wonder if it is time to quit teaching. Martin Luther suggested that a person teach for seven years at most. I've been at it for over eighteen, far too long.

Finishing the semester, there's only graduation left to endure, facing angry parents, priests, and ministers.

This year graduation is on a Saturday, not the usual Sunday. No one knows why.

I'm sitting with the other ducks in my academic robes (this time my memory worked), listening to graduation speeches and wondering if I'll ever teach again. No parents attack me, and there are no angry clergy in sight.

That night in a dream, I'm in Rome speaking fluent Italian; the words just flowed naturally. In waking life, I can only speak the language easily when I've been drinking beer—and now, apparently, dreaming.

The dream: On the Spanish Steps, I'm talking to a monk—don't know the order—about the modern quest of the historical Jesus. He's an old man, thin and wiry, yet he argues vigorously. And the sunlight is peeking over the buildings, heating the ancient stones and masonry as if they're warm bread, and I feel really healthy for the first time in many years.

I have no idea how the argument goes or who the monk was; it simply fades away as I come to wakefulness.

Thinking about the dream, I once more experience that terrible body chill associated with kidney failure. Since the administration of EPO in dialysis, I'd forgotten this particular symptom. Every point my hematocrit rises is like another log on the fire. But for years, I'd tried to ignore it, a constant cold that no amount of clothes could chase away. It went far too deep.

The dream makes me remember, and I'm thankful for dialysis, thankful for the medical profession, for the nurses. Bless them. They are truly angels.

The dream lingers for days. I resist analyzing it. Some things should remain a mystery, to be enjoyed as such.

Ah, but the past can never be recaptured. This I know. Perhaps Buddha had it right: Dependent origination, everything arises from multiple influences. And who can know the subtle differences between yesterday and today? Such things as the quality of the air, the difference in sunlight between our time and the ancient world, the variations in water, pressure, plants, animals, and a thousand other things. I remember being struck in places like Athens and Rome by the smell. Antiquity has a certain odor.

I've never truly appreciated these wonders until this time, as I've come to the edge of darkness. It is remarkable, beautiful. Bless my illness!

# ↢ 27 ↣

# Whom Nature Made

(Dante, Purgatorio, Canto 29)

What joy to come home after dialysis and not have to play Professor—but to come home and recover from the rigors of treatment. What bliss! Here's one thing Joseph Campbell neglected when he pontificated about "bliss." Bliss is being able to rest after dialysis—just as the Buddha forgot the ninth path.

That afternoon, inspired by my missionary student (divine inspiration?), I take a little journey to the local Christian bookstore, where I pick up the creationist classic, *Bones of Contention* by Marvin Lubenow. He's very good. He goes after all the questionable dating, the fossil identification problems, geology, solar science, the Big Bang—everything. He even strikes out at the Old Testament sources theory: Moses wrote and signed the Pentateuch, says Lubenow, although he doesn't explain how Moses wrote his own death scene into Deuteronomy—a major miracle if there ever was one.

From hints in the text, I take it that Lubenow roams about the country, debating evolutionists (as he calls them), and most of the time comes out on top.

Monkeys of the world unite!

Was the flood local or worldwide? Worldwide, says Lubenow (he's serious too). I wonder about the Gilgamesh flood. Some of his supporters hold doctorates in the sciences from major universities. They want to take evolution out of everything: physics, cosmology, geology, as well as biology. They're quietly eroding grade school and high school science texts, working through local school boards. This method proves more fruitful than the old and failed legal attempts to bring creation science into the curriculum.

Creation science reminds me of German physics during the Third Reich. Professor Philipp Lenard and his Aryan followers founded an Association of Aryan Physicists to combat Einstein's Jewish physics, which was Lenard's name for relativity. Einstein himself would sneak into their meetings and have a good laugh.

The Nazis attempted to build a nuclear weapon ($E=MC^2$). Apparently, Jewish physics became Aryan physics when used to build atomic bombs for the Reich.

Lubenow keeps asking for links. This question alone seems to indicate that he really hasn't grasped natural selection: *Every species is a link.* He says that the newer forms of an animal cannot be contemporary with ancestral forms. But this is clearly false since geological barriers often separate species. He claims evolution is fueled by death, hence its ideology is death and destruction. But extinction is not the engine of evolution. Evolution is powered by differential reproduction, the ability of a species to produce *more* young.

Lubenow insists on frozen Platonic forms—his idea of the species—rather than fluid process and irreversible change. But every form is a bridge, a link, in motion to something else, which no one, even God, can foresee in this universe of indeterminacy (Heisenberg, chaos theory, my damned fistula).

Should we teach the Bible's creation myth to children in public school? Most definitely. I find my students woefully ignorant of the Hebrew scriptures, the founding documents of our civilization. But we need to teach other creation epics as well. I especially like one from the Upanishads: In the beginning there is the One Being (Sat), and the One splits into two, male and female, and he pursues her, and she changes into a mare, and he a stallion, and they copulate as such . . . and so it goes, one after another, *all the forms of nature*. In every form they have sex—thousands of species, thousands of copulations, for thousands of years. Thus is divinity infused into all nature. We are all sons and daughters of God.

I know this fear that drives Lubenow. I know this terrible yet awesome Heraclitean river. I've seen it flow past. No matter medical science, I shall *never* recapture health. Even the transplant is a roll of the dice, a treatment, not a cure. That world has flowed away. Such is the essence of the Buddha's First Noble Truth.

～

Maxwell stops by for a visit. He whispers in my ear: "That thing in your chest is oozing something . . ."

I tell the charge nurse, who then takes a sample of the "something" and ships the sample to the lab. Meanwhile I'm placed on antibiotics.

Since the tubes grow out of my heart, an infection in the catheter could destroy the heart muscle, and I'd require a heart transplant too!

The antibiotics seem to work. The ooze goes away in a week. There's no fever. My new fistula hums along, maturing. Neo Tubes work so well that I'm running at rates heretofore unapproachable. A PR, we used to say in track—personal record.

And meanwhile Maxwell is waiting.

# Part VI

# Darth Neardeath

# ☙ 28 ❧

# The Short Race

(Dante, Purgatorio, Canto 20)

Adjusting to the tubes, learning to live with them, is far more depressing than anything the social worker could imagine. The tubes are a constant reminder that I'm truly ill, living this half-life, a marginal man. Usually when the fistula band-aids came off in the afternoon of a treatment day, I could ignore the puncture wounds in my arm, even joke about my stigmata. But the dangling tubes are a continuous mocking reminder. The catheter tube, leading down into the heart, is clearly visible through the flesh as it passes over the collarbone. I'm afraid of hitting it when I shave.

In clinic, the nurses seem friendlier and more ready to talk. Hooking me up to the machine is a snap. Anybody can do it, even the nurses in training. Anybody can screw in two connecting nozzles without screwing up.

So, the job is easier for them, but I'm forced into new routines, like taking sponge baths instead of showers, since soaking the bandages might cause infections. Naturally, the tubes need to be taped firmly before a run.

The fear of reappearing ooze requires constant examination of the wounds, hence awareness of the condition. Unlike Neo in *The Matrix*, no Morpheus comes to rescue me.

Yet, the nurses are there, willing to talk. Mean-looking-but-gentle Vicki never forsakes me, but now her friend Jean—blonde, red-faced, rather stout—cautiously approaches, always in Vicki's company. One day, not really intending anything funny, I refer to them as "Tweedle-dee and Tweedle-dum." They instantly dissolve into laughter, then tears. Never have they heard any-thing so funny. Before long, the unintended joke spreads through the clinic, like an infection.

Encouraged, I try to be funny.

"Hey Tweedle-dee and Tweedle-dum." Laughter. "There's a man from the island of Crete who says that all Cretans are liars. Is he telling the truth?"

Silence. Jean chews on her lip. Vicki looks angry.

"Uh . . . the Roman writer Pliny once wondered if God could commit suicide?"

Vicki mutters: "God can do anything."

Laughing, I respond: "That's the point. If He can, how can He still be God, since the Absolute is unchangeable and impassable and can't be killed? But if He can't, how can He be God since all things are possible to the deity?"

The consensus is: Not funny!

Once, a researcher visited a grade school in Austria, where the philosopher Ludwig Wittgenstein had taught. The towns-folk and former students remembered the philosopher. They also remembered the lying Cretan paradox. Should some future scholar come to the dialysis clinic, he or she will probably hear of the Tweedle-dee, Tweedle-dum paradox.

∼

Ramona, the African-American nurse, tall with striking features, about thirty, has seemingly taken a liking to me (but I can never be sure in this toxin saturated state).

She had talked to me previously, but now for some reason—another blessing of the tubes—she decides it's safe to joke and tease. Mostly we talk about her problems with men, her problems with friends and parents, her problems with her. Almost every day she wears a different hairdo, sometimes of different colors, usually wigs.

"You're trying to find yourself, Ramona. You don't know who you are. . . . Perhaps you don't want to know, so you wear masks."

I'm joking, but she takes it very seriously. "I'm just tryin' out different looks!"

"Nope. Masks. Who are you really?"

"You're the strangest patient we've ever had."

This I take as a compliment.

Later, Big Daddy comes over and asks what I've done to Ramona.

Ramona is the toughest nurse in the clinic. The buddhas would try to flirt with her and she'd take them down with ease. Even Big Daddy himself treated her with a certain wariness.

"Nothing. Just a little joke."

"Well, she's after you now."

It's true. I tell her that the whole thing was a joke, but she remains skeptical. One day we're talking about running; I'm giving advice about workouts, injuries, shoes, and talking about my own exploits (how hard it is to really practice the Buddha's dharma of non-self!).

"Let's go for a run together," she suggests.

"Fine. How about five miles tomorrow afternoon?"

The instant agreement must have taken her by surprise. Obviously, she thinks I'm bragging, exaggerating—that a dialysis patient couldn't run a single mile.

She seems even more surprised when I show up the following afternoon. I meet her at a local trail, having run a mile and a half to get there. We start off at what seems to me an easy jog, and before we've gone a half mile, she's forced to walk.

Next day, I tell Big Daddy the tale and in an hour, it has spread through the clinic.

Ramona comes along and once again shakes her head. "You are the *weirdest patient* we've ever had." Now, however, she's laughing.

Of course, all of this occurs in a fog. Sometimes it seems that a person's sensitivity, empathy, awareness of those subtle forms of human communication, the dichotomies of interaction, are filtered out with the toxins. How much is fantasy? Reality? Where does the dream end and the waking begin, as old Schopenhauer asked long ago?

Yet, the jokes, the teasing, could all be a form of aggression, the result of frustrations arising from illness. And if the frustrations become unbearable, one could easily desire annihilation. Perhaps this is why Buddhism with its doctrine of emptiness and anatman has become so appealing. Yet, we all suffer from this, as the First Noble Truth suggests. Our goals, the things we acquire (status, wealth, power), are all subject to decay, or simply become boring and stale over time. Ultimately, a deeper frustration emerges as everything shows itself as forms of emptiness. "Form is emptiness, emptiness is not different from form." Yet, the statement is optimistic. If form was not empty, how could I change?

Here I stand consumed with self. Once again, illness inflates the self into an all-encompassing universe. Another battle is lost; unreflective habits, built from craving, frustration, clinging, have eaten into my personality.

Even this train of thought is evidence of self-obsession, and so, too, this memoir.

Kidney failure is only part of the struggle.

~

Today I come off the machine with one of those skull-pounding headaches, this one from low blood pressure. The experience of my first shave may have contributed to it.

The hair had begun to grow beneath the catheter bandage. My nurse for the day is a little thing named Dorothy (giggle, giggle). Dorothy has been nursing for about a year. She "just loves" dialysis work because it keeps her occupied and yet is not as stressful as the hospital. Nurse Dorothy is not allowed to stick patients. Yet. Soon, however, she will be. I pray to whatever gods happen to be listening that I'm not around when she does.

Dorothy gets to meet "many interesting people" in clinic. Most patients are friendly; some of the males tease her; she "just loves" it here. She watches *Oprah* whenever she is able.

As she talks, she lathers my chest, and then produces a regular barber's razor, pearl handle and all.

"Careful with my tit!" I cry out in alarm.

"Oh!" Giggle giggle.

~

Vicki, the old veteran, tells me the story of a guy named Walter. Walter was a prisoner brought to the dialysis clinic by two guards whose job was to stand and watch the machine clean Walter's blood.

Walter was in for life. He'd killed his mother, stabbing her through the eye with a sharp pencil. Walter would write letters during treatment. But these letters were filled with nonsense sentences and addressed to nonexistent people. He wrote with a pencil.

Once, Vicki missed his access and gave him a huge hema-tomato. He flew into a rage, gripping his pencil hard. At that moment, the guards were flirting with the nurses; Vicki thought that she was done for. But Walter allowed her to live.

She used to sit and hold his wounds after extracting the needles. While they waited for the bleeding to stop, he would impatiently tap his pencil on the pad of paper. Vicki feared that one day he'd suddenly stab her in the eye. He never did.

Walter died after having a stroke on the machine.

I'm watching her, as if really seeing Vicki for the first time: the skin creases, the tired eyes, the habitual frown, the wariness. Dialysis nursing is a job, true, but suddenly I perceive the sacrifices, the burdens, the largely unappreciated care she gives—all of them give. And I feel a deep sense of shame at how blind I've become, so cocooned in my illness, living in my books, that I can't recognize Buddha or Jesus when she appears.

# ⇐ 29 ⇒

# The Force

(Dante, Purgatorio, Canto 25)

It's the middle of May, a late Sunday afternoon, sunny and hot. We're on the soccer fields for a tournament, awaiting the start of the championship game in which Sophia will start at the striker position.

Suddenly my transplant beeper begins bleating. It shows a number. Sutra Cindi is calling.

My heart nearly squeezes out of the tubes. I run for the nearest pay phone and dial her number.

*"We have a kidney offer, Anthony."* She's not sure I'll want it. The match is only one out of six, and worse, there's a "surgical risk." The kidney comes from a child, and small kidneys generally fail when placed into an adult. While she didn't think I'd say yes, protocol demands that she call anyway.

I tell her to give it to a child on dialysis, since kids don't get adult organs.

Shaken, dazed, I walk back to the game. Hardly able to focus on the action, I suddenly realize that as my child and hundreds of others on these fields play soccer, somewhere *another child has just died.* The sadness is overwhelming. Cheeks glistening, my eyes begin to sting. The children I'm watching suddenly become luminous, like torches burning fiercely in their transience.

I think about Dostoevsky's novel A *Raw Youth*: A couple loses their children in an accident, and a group of friends try to decide what would balance their loss. And then one voice, surely from *The House of the Dead*, asserts that the only proper response is to somehow return their loved ones to them. The children must absolutely be alive. All else is gesture.

And I recall that story in Chekhov where a cab driver's son has died in the afternoon and all through the night he keeps trying to tell his wealthy fares what has happened, but instead is required to listen to their little problems with pets and such banalities. On the way back to the barn, all alone, he speaks of his pain to his horse.

And even the among the ancients. After his only daughter died, the Roman writer Cicero sought answers to the tragedy by writing a dialogue *Of the Nature of the Gods*. Are there gods who watch over us, Cicero wondered? Coming to the end, he sighs and says: "What an obscure point it is, and with what difficulties an explanation of it is attended."

All else is gesture. Such things are happening every moment. For the first time I find it nearly impossible to bear the suffering, and my own illness has nothing to do with this feeling.

Sophia's team has lost the game, yet it doesn't matter. I hug her tightly . . . which she thinks is for consolation . . . and she's right.

~

The nurses want to know if I've seen the new *Star Wars* movie, the *Phantom Menace*.

"Of course. I have three kids."

"Did you like it?"

"The phantom movie?"

Vicki snickers. By now she knows what's coming.

Yakob and I had already discussed the movie, so toxins or not I was prepared.

"Well, needless to say, I was the only one in the theater who laughed when the storyline scrolled into the far horizon, announcing that the war was because of a tariff! And talk about violence. Mayhem start to finish. And no acting either. Lucas must forbid it on his sets. The machines star. And the aliens—the bad ones—sound like they originally spoke Chinese and learned English in a mission school."

Tweedle-dee and Tweedle-dum think this funny; the others are frowning.

"And George Rip-off! The Naboo city looked like Dinotopia; the undersea city like *The Abyss*. The planet-wide city that serves as the Republic's capital is taken from Asimov's *Foundation*. Hey, did you catch it when Anikan's mom said that her little Darth-to-be had no father? The Hebrew savior on another planet, like C. S. Lewis. Darth Mall looked like Satan for sure." I spell Mall.

"Isn't it M-a-u-l?" asks Jean.

"Mall. A joke on merchants perhaps? Oh no, George would never risk a funny. Did you note that his world seems to exist free of sex? Goodness and boredom appear linked in George's mind."

The nurses, even Vicki and Jean, quickly find other things that urgently require their attention.

But the movie did disappoint. Now we're told that there's some chemical in the blood that blesses the Jedi with the ability to use the Force. The bad guys, like the Darths, must have it too, since they're good turned evil. The rest of the herd, us, must possess only traces. Sounds like Nazi racial theories. Good Nazis, bad Nazis, the servant class.

Maybe George knows that his Oprahized audience would find any mystical interpretation too difficult—fantasy for the *Oprah* set with its increasingly limited attention span. No one is challenged.

Yakob says that there's an entry in a volume of Thomas Merton's journals. It is the end of June 1964, and Merton is in New York City, and meets D. T. Suzuki, then ninety-four years old. Suzuki tells him that Paul Tillich liked the Zen tea ceremony (green tea consumed in three-and-a-half sips as prescribed), but didn't like the German mystic Meister Eckhart. A heretic! says Tillich.

I laugh to myself. He would have approved of the phantom movie. Suzuki insists upon love more than enlightenment in Buddhism. "We are all different expressions of the same emptiness."

Merton concludes: "We both agreed on the need to steer clear of movements and to avoid promoting Zen or anything else."

∽

Ramona has just spent a good hour telling me about her problems with men. He's got to be rich, she says, otherwise forget it. She'd even go for being a trophy wife.

I try to argue with her, that this sort of marriage is a kind of legalized prostitution. Along the way, I toss in my old joke that teaching is mental prostitution, but rather dull and boring compared to the somatic kind. She ignores this and continues on about financial security. But my blood pressure is dropping, and arguments for the spiritual, the finer, romance-as-an-art, more human qualities of marriage begin to sound ridiculous as opposed to her practical, impregnable materialism. Maxwell is fiddling with that damned door again.

She leaves. Materialism is the winner. And what wouldn't I give, not for the Force blood cells, but that humble gene that provides the normal regulation of blood pressure?

# ⤚ 30 ⤛

# Like Things Twice Dead

(Dante, Purgatorio, Canto 24)

I've always loved running in the heat and humidity. Misha the malamute, my running partner, naturally hates it. So I leave him home in the air conditioning and run alone. But now the bandage covering my chest is soaking wet and heavy, threatening to fall off. Blood pressure is lower now as well. Coming into treatment my pressure is 102/60, and during dialysis, it plummets. Suddenly it's 80/50, then 70/35. . . . Again, words melt on the page, the room spins in a smoky fog, and my heart begins to race (ventricular tachycardia, progressing to fibrillation, or what nurses call Code Blue, DEAD). From somewhere far away, I hear myself calling out for help.

Ramona pumps in the saline and once again saves my life.

I'm feeling much stronger not having to teach, and it is possible that I've gained some weight. But in dialysis, my weight gain is perceived as a fluid gain, and the ultrafiltration rate is raised to dry me out. And since I'm dehydrated from running, every treatment becomes a near-death experience. Darth Neardeath.

This third Monday in June I come down with a hundred-and-three fever. The day is warm and humid, yet I'm so chilled that I bury myself under mounds of blankets, shaking as if suffering a seizure. The chills last for hours and then are followed by sweating and overheating.

It is a long, sleepless night.

The next morning, Tuesday, Dr. Jung orders me to the clinic. One of my upper arm incisions bulges with pus. Dr. Jung decides that the wound is infected. Bacteria got in through the sutures and into my blood. He prescribes a powerful dose of antibiotics.

Swallowing the first tablet, I instantly feel better.

Until . . .

On Wednesday during treatment, my blood pressure takes another dive into the abyss. That afternoon the fever makes a triumphant return. Feeling really sick, nauseated, and weak, I place all my hope in the antibiotics.

However, life must go on. I drag myself to the grocery store with Sophia. It is another hot and sun-drenched day. As we enter the store, a blast of cold air hits us like a fist. Instantly I begin to shake.

I should have walked out right there! But if we could just get out of the frozen food section, perhaps the chills would subside. After all, illness must not be allowed to interfere with such an important activity as grocery shopping.

The chills don't go away. They intensify, and transform into shivering, then teeth-rattling shaking. Sophia begins to panic, but I tell her that everything is fine, just a chill from the freezers. Despite every bit of will power I can muster, every yoga exercise, every breathing discipline—pleas to every god I know—the shaking gets worse. The shaking is so bad that it is impossible to take products off the shelves. Making a game out of it—you do this, I do that—I trick Sophia into filling the cart herself. She also unloads the products in the checkout line. Writing the check to pay for the groceries is agony, but not because of the cost. The thing is completely illegible. Yet, they take it without question.

In this culture—grocery store, not culture—being unable to shop is the surest sign that the end is near, Neardeath. And in Dante's capitalist *Inferno*, such a sin earns one the deepest level of the pit. Money has replaced oath breaking.

Somehow we make it to the car. Sophia, knowing that something is seriously wrong, tearfully unloads the groceries. That I drive home is a major miracle. We have the car heater on full blast, the windows rolled up, and it's nearly ninety degrees outside.

An hour later and I'm back in the clinic. It's Thursday, and once again, I feel deep sympathy for the nurses who spend every day here.

They sit me in the usual blue chair and drain gallons of blood from my tubes. For two hours, they pump in a steady stream of antibiotics.

Dr. Jung comes in and pronounces me septic. He doesn't need to see the cultures. So it's official. In the course of his examination of my chest stigmata, he notices that one of the nozzles, the threaded end of the tube, is *cracked!* Eight weeks of hooking the tubes to the machine and no one caught it.

Instantly a call is made to the hospital. *The catheter must be pulled.* Dialysis must now be done through my new fistula, ready or not. The catheter is breeding bacteria like an ant farm. If the infection goes to my heart, with the faulty mitral valve, I'll need *two* transplants.

~

Sick with fever, still quaking like a scared rabbit, I somehow drive to the hospital. By luck, I've brought the correct insurance cards. Admissions is, this time, a minor
ordeal. What would have happened had I forgotten
them? Would they send me away with this fever (now
about one hundred four)? What about others with worse
problems? Do administrators have a conscience? I *know*
the answer in terms of higher education. Perhaps hospital
administrators are different.

I'm led to a consulting room. Three people enter, one
a real doctor, the two others his apprentices. The master,
brusque and seemingly irritated, takes a look at my chest
and then *asks me what needs to be done!*

"Pull the damned tubes!"

He nods and barks out orders to his apprentices, then
leaves the room.

Now I'm truly frightened. The nightmare of every
professor: left alone in the hands of students!

They make me lie down on the table. One freezes
the site with injections of lidocaine, while the other
approaches with an instrument that resembles silver pliers. This, he says, will be used to spread the skin around
the catheter.

"You'll feel a little pressure."

Feeling a little pressure, translated from medicalese,
means, "It's going to hurt like hell."

My head is back on the pillow and I can't see what
he's doing. He seems to be digging deep into my chest,
very deep. Suddenly he grasps the catheter's cuff with
another pair of pliers and begins to pull. The tube, don't
forget, *reaches down into my heart vein.*

And I can feel it, like a burning in the chest after eating chili peppers.

Jesusmaryjosephandallthesaints . . . and Oprah, and Deepak, and Sutra Cindi . . . anybody!

His face is contorted with the effort. He gives a good yank, then another.

Brahmashivavishnuandkrishna . . .

The remains of whatever dignity I once possessed have now dissolved into wordless gasps and moans, and other animal-like noises.

Suddenly both are busy with gauze. Then they seem occupied with their instruments.

Minutes pass. Finally, I meekly inquire: "Well?"

"What?"

"Is it out?"

"Yeah. Been out for some time. Thought you knew."

"No."

"Well, you were easy. We pulled out a catheter this afternoon that had been in for two years. Took us an hour. Lots of yankin' and pullin', a real problem."

"Should have used a winch," I observe. They both laugh.

Bandaged up, I'm finally released and sent home. The two apprentices wish me good luck with my new fistula.

~

Once the catheter is gone I feel better. No more fever, no more shakes or freezing in the middle of summer.

Next treatment, when the blood cultures come back from the lab, it turns out that there were *two* species of bugs in my blood, one a rather deadly critter known to take away the elderly. But the antibiotics they gave me through IV didn't work on either. They were the wrong drugs for these bugs. Dr. Jung orders some new drugs even though I'm fever-free.

The corpsman comes and very carefully sticks the new fistula. Both of us hold our breath. The needles slide in, he makes the connections to the machine, starts the pump, the tubes turn red. . . .

It works.

While I was sick with septicemia, a well-matched kidney was "harvested." But with the infection, they passed me over. I feel some regret, yet at this moment I'm quite content to be alive, even if on dialysis.

Rejection medicines would have killed me and the new kidney. I'll need to wait a few weeks before being placed back on the list. None of this seems as important as my new working fistula.

~

Death, that dread antagonist, once more appeared at my door. Maxwell's door. With the aid of modern medicine, I've been able to hold the fort against him (her, it). What have I learned?

I have learned that death is hateful, as Homer says in the *Iliad*. When the heroes die—Patroclus, Hector, many more before the gates of Troy—Homer repeats:

> Death cut him short. The end closed in around him.
>
> Flying free of his limbs
>
> his soul went winging down to the House of Death,
>
> wailing his fate, leaving his manhood far behind,
>
> his young and subtle strength.

I have learned that people place death into a hidden compartment, locked firmly away. And I've acted no differently.

I have learned that death is frightening in its unpredictability, its irreversibility, in the rational probability that it all ends there, in that hateful dark, as Homer says.

I have learned that religion has its roots deep in that hateful place.

And yet, having acknowledged all this, I have learned too that death is a kind of illusion built from the iron bonds of self. Attachment to illusion breeds fear and loathing, as the Buddha knew. Perhaps illness teaches this lesson to those willing to listen. The healthy self died, replaced by this dialysis self. The self is always dying, somehow, and this continual change is frightening. So, we grasp hopelessly for stability, for Platonic absolutes, which are themselves illusions, and it becomes a vicious circle.

Nothing very profound here. However, despite the dread, the gloom, and the terror, something has changed. Perhaps I've acquired a gut feeling, a new sense if you will, that there's nothing unnatural or evil about death. I've said such things previously, but those words were abstract, from the intellect. Now they arise from the earth.

Death is not some flaw in creation (although much that I've said elsewhere seems to imply that it is), not some dark invader caused by human folly. It is surely not the wages of human sin, some poison administered to a previously deathless creation—and tell me, Monsieur l'Abbé, what is "spiritual death"? Nor is it a punishment administered by some leering, angry, and cruel god. No.

Death is natural enough, is nature, is the other side of life's coin. From this perspective, in fact, *death is life*.

When one is healthy, full of life, anticipating more life, then death is feared—as Homer says, hateful. But as the toxins soaked into my cells and the dreadful fatigue froze my limbs, chilling my body, death no longer seemed frightening. It appeared to be the intrinsic end of a progression, nothing to blame on anyone or anything.

According to legend, the Buddha came to a small village where he was confronted by a woman holding a recently deceased child. The woman begged him to bring her child back to life (here, perhaps, is the answer to Dostoevsky).

"I will restore the child," said the Blessed One, "but first you must do something for me. Bring me a mustard seed from a single house in this village that has not experienced death."

Yes, the smallest of seeds, and also a great weed. Could this realization be what Jesus meant by the Kingdom of God?

# ≈ 31 ≈

# Daniel

(DANTE, PURGATORIO, CANTO 22)

Maxwell had opened another door to yet one more unsuspected dialysis experience. The frequency of a fistula simply shutting down as mine did is about two percent. It was an accident of your anatomy, Dr. Jung explained; the vein was too narrow near the inner elbow and finally shut off. An accident of anatomy. . . .

Today, my new fistula gave a good spurt of blood with the first stick. But then Nurse Dorothy decided to hit a nerve with the venous needle. Naturally, I responded with inappropriate language, another set of lyrics for my rap song about the clinic. Because most of the nerves in my upper arm are undamaged, I can look forward to many more such experiences.

After treatment, the inside of my right arm has turned an amazing shade of bright blue, nearly matching the chair. Such a color seems hardly possible in live human flesh. No matter how many hema-tomatoes the old fistula withstood, it never looked like this. A little more and I could be mistaken for Krishna, the blue-boy god of Hindu mythology and the *Bhagavad Gita*.

Meanwhile, the patients and some of the nurses are watching a doctor on one of the morning TV shows. He wrote a book about preventing aging (he himself looks older than mud). He advises the patients and nurses not to eat fast food! This is a revelation? His book is a best seller.

Today is also Ramona's last day. She's moving to a bigger city and a better dialysis clinic. I suddenly realize that I'll miss her.

Our final conversation is about religion, which, to my surprise, was her doing. But once more, I'm faced with the rather odd assumption that if one doesn't accept the Christian god one doesn't believe in God at all. Tongue-in-cheek, I argue for other options, polytheism for example.

"Many gods?"

"Yeah. The more gods the merrier."

"That's crazy!"

"Is it? With many gods, the poor human can play one god off against the other, and get away in between. Like: Hey YHWH, did you hear what Zeus said about you?"

"You're weird. I'll pray for you Sunday."

"No! Don't do that, please. Don't bring me to *His* attention. I'm quite happy when He ignores me."

She frowns, but then starts to laugh.

I'll miss Ramona.

∼

Samantha, the dialysis coordinator, walked into the clinic today, a hot Wednesday in July. I wave to her with my free hand, but she's busy with other patients. Her job is patient education, preparing people technically and psychologically for the ordeal of dialysis. It was her task from the first day I met her in Dr. Jung's office to make certain I started treatments when the toxin numbers soared too high. She might be called an expert in denial.

In her office, listening to all the good reasons why dialysis should begin, one gets the feeling that she is taking a personal interest. Perhaps the toxins were already fogging my perception.

As it became apparent, to everyone but me, that my kidneys would fail, our meetings became more frequent. Little by little, she dismantled my fortress of resistance, beguiling me with warmth and concern. And this fortress, constructed with the stone and mortar of past experience, rationalizations, and skepticism—"but quantum mechanics says"—seemed impregnable. Samantha deconstructed it with ease.

She led me to believe that I was a special case, seemingly spending more time with me than others. Once she missed a meeting. I've used students to miss faculty meetings. Why couldn't I see the maneuver from a different angle? She convinced me to submit to the first fistula, made me promise her that I'd begin treatment when the time came. Not keeping this promise would have been like betrayal. She was very good at manipulation, an artist.

And today, since I've been a good boy, she's on to the next patient.

Soberly I realize that I was never anything but another patient. How stupid to think otherwise. Samantha was doing her job. Perhaps it even bored her. In the economic scheme of things, I was a product of her labor. Patients, like students, are products.

I laugh to myself. If I were healthy, I might be angry for being duped so easily. Now I'm only sad in a humorous, ironic way. Marx might have called it the fetish of commodities, the patient-product, one like the next. Value in capitalism is not a personal relationship, as Adam Smith said of the butcher in *The Wealth of Nations*.

And have I not done the same with students? Are they not student-products of higher education? So once again, illness is the great teacher, its lesson being empathy and perspective. How fortunate to have kidney failure!

～

Two rows from my machine, the old man named Danny is moaning again. Two hours into treatment and he begins to moan and curse. And for him, poor soul, two hours is halftime.

"Goddammit, Goddammit, take me off. Oh why, oh why . . ."

A few nurses are sympathetic and attempt to console him. Others seem to enjoy the diversion: "Sorry, Danny, you've got two more hours to go. Can't let you out now."

Telling him the time remaining is especially cruel.

"Oh please, oh please . . . Son of a bitch!"

They scold him. "No one else is complaining. Be quiet!"

"Oh why, oh why . . ." He goes on for at least thirty minutes, until he's exhausted.

I feel like moaning and cursing just to prove them wrong, and demonstrate camaraderie.

Meanwhile, the new fistula is working far better than the old, so I shut my mouth lest the gods hear. But I'm still a hard stick, because the fistula forms a Z on my upper arm, making it easy to go clean through with the big needles. Shorter needles, however, seem to work.

By the end of summer, I've reached a kind of stasis. This morning, however, preparing for treatment I take a good look at the mirror: graying hair, sunken eyes, haggard facial lines, emaciated body—single chin and a single wit, to paraphrase Shakespeare. Growing weaker, little by little, it's a slow death in place of a quicker one.

# ≈ 32 ≈

# Wolf or Hound

(DANTE, PURGATORIO, CANTO 27)

I think daily about death. I feel the randomness of things, the contingency and transience of my existence. These thoughts are not depressing, not morbid. They seem, well, funny. Absolutes, the "truth," seem far too serious and stern when gazed upon from the rollicking dialysis chair. However, randomness appears very real. Failed kidneys and all, I live on this planet by chance, not some divine plan.

At such times I think, too, about Dostoevsky's character in *The Brothers Karamazov*, the older brother of the Elder Zosima, named Markel. Markel went to the university and lost his faith. Fasting during Lent, he told his mother, giving her quite a shock, is "delirium . . . because there is no God."

But then one Lent, Markel became seriously ill. The illness grew worse, and ultimately, was fatal.

With this illness came his own kind of delirium: He'd say crazy things like "Life is a paradise although we don't want to see it."

Dostoevsky then goes on to relate Markel's final days:

> When the doctor came—an old German called Eisenschmidt—Markel would ask him: "Tell me,

doctor, will I be one more day in this world?" He always joked with the doctor, who would answer: "It's not a question of a day, or even many days. You'll be here for many months and years yet . . ."

"There's no need for years or even months, days are enough; a single day is sufficient for a man to discover what happiness is. Why must we quarrel, brag, and remember offenses against us? Why shouldn't we go into the garden right now and love, kiss, praise, and enjoy one another, and bless our lives?" When mother saw the doctor off, he said to her: "I'm afraid your son is not long for this world— his illness has affected his brain now." . . . He died in the third week after Easter. . . . He looked happy and there was a spark of joy in his eyes.

I ponder this passage as I run in the summer of 1999, the season of life, and the turning of the millennium. We are told that Markel, before he died, had even asked the little birds outside his window to forgive him.

It is true. A single day lived in such a way is enough. I've had many days, months, years. But have I lived them as Markel did when he was ill?

≈

Misha. Sophia and Anna grew up with him. Anna used to ride on his back and fall asleep between his paws. A big dog, he weighed about one hundred ten pounds.

Misha was my running companion. For most of his life, he accompanied me on our daily afternoon run. He was always ready to go; often he got me going as the illness drained my energy. When it came to pass that I could barely lift my miserable carcass out of my chair, Misha was there, eagerly urging me on.

Misha looked like a wolf. As we passed, children would ask: "Is that a wolf?" Once, a little boy, fear in his voice, cried out: "Look, mommy, the big bad wolf!" "Oh no," I replied, laughing, "he's not the big bad wolf. He's the big baby."

I often wondered if Misha were afraid of the dark. On those bleak winter evenings, when dusk arrives a little after four, we'd run side by side and he seemed to always brush a little closer to me as the light faded. I worried that Misha lacked even the "normal" dog intelligence. He seemed trainable to a limit. Once he ran headlong into a red fire hydrant and knocked himself unconscious. He came when called—sometimes—when it amused him, apparently. He was always hungry and especially liked that delicacy, deer droppings.

Once when working on his yard fence, Misha sneaked up behind, grabbed a pair of pliers, and ran like the wind. I was furious; later I laughed. The tool never turned up.

Perhaps he was more stubborn than dumb, a fiercely independent creature who chose to live with us and run with me.

Those final years, pressed by that terrible chill and fatigue, Misha and I seemed to grow closer. We still ran. He dragged me down the road. But he, too, grew older, and he slept more, mainly next to my chair, where I dozed in the semiconsciousness of kidney failure.

Armine called him a sweet dog. The kids wrestled with him and never would he growl. He even tolerated the cat.

～

One hot July evening in 1999, we found Misha at the bottom of the hill in his yard. He was stretched out in the mud, panting. For the past few days, his appetite had not been at its usually voracious level. We blamed it on the heat and kept him in air conditioning.

There was no improvement. We took him to the vet. The verdict was diabetes! Misha would require two shots of insulin daily. Like me, he would be impaled, Vlad the Impaled's hound.

His appetite and energy did seem to improve, but only a little. In a week, he'd become progressively weaker, barely able to drag himself outside in the evening, like me before dialysis.

We took him back to the vet and discovered that Misha had an infection. Now we had to mix antibiotics with his food. Yet, he ate less and less.

~

On Sunday, we found that Misha could not get to his feet. Luc and I sat with him for most of the day, vainly trying to get antibiotics down his throat. He watched us as if from far away. I thought that I could see the wolf in those eyes, and behind, the dark pine forests of the northlands. I apologized, asked him to forgive us for bringing him here.

His temperature continued to climb. We heaved him into a tub of cold water. Finally, although it was late Sunday afternoon, we took him to the animal hospital. We had to lift him in and out of the car. His limbs were limp, his head lolled.

The vets took blood and gave him IV fluids. We stayed at his side. He appeared to improve, and they said they'd keep him for a day. At last we left, telling each other that Misha would be fine.

About eleven that evening the phone rang. Naturally I thought it was a kidney. Not this time.

Misha had died.

~

I stand alone in the backyard, expecting to see Misha come loping up the hill, ready for a run, a wolf emerging from the forest. In philosophy, we are told that language can create experience; for me, at this moment, words are too feeble to capture experience. Words are so flimsy, that broken and torn net through which experience passes and escapes.

An old farmer, a heart patient, told Armine that he was through with dogs. He'd had four. All of them died. "It just tears your heart out every time," he said.

And standing there, feeling worse than any dialysis treatment, I suddenly recall a run with Misha. We ran side by side, both of us still healthy and filled with the joy of health. It was a warm spring day, and we came to a sparkling fountain. Misha jumped upon the low brick wall to have a drink. He was perched on the narrow ridge, but its surface was slick and he lost his balance. With a crazy flurry of paws and tail, he plunged into the fountain, making a huge splash. In a panic, he paddled about and finally dragged himself out of the water.

He shook off and glared at me, apparently holding me responsible for this terrible indignity.

"It's not my fault," I told him, and laughed. It is no one's fault, this innocence of chance.

# ❧ 33 ❧

# The Music of the Spheres

(DANTE, PURGATORIO, CANTO 30)

A bright day in early December 1999, I'm sitting quietly in a classroom giving a final exam. The pain in
my upper arm is a dull reminder of the morning's dialysis.
Pretending to watch the students, I am really staring out
the windows, admiring the clear, crisp, empty sky. Then a
strange thing happens.

My mental stream ceases to flow; thought suddenly
evaporates. Nothing changed: the sky, the classroom,
perspiring students. But abruptly there is no "I," only
experience. A great peace settles upon the scene, a vast
stillness as if a river has suddenly ceased running. Emptiness opens, and yet emptiness is also fullness: Trees,
brown grass, patches of snow, sky and sun, buildings,
desks, students, but I have departed.

Pain melts like a patch of snow beneath the sun.
Nausea goes on holiday. Time becomes a spatial dimen-
sion, and only the now remains, like the frozen dimensions of the table. Perception is never more vivid.

A student comes up to my table with a question
about the exam. I do not respond. The question-about-
a-question is repeated. Nothing. A third time, now with
mild annoyance.

The water begins to flow again. The noise outside, the chatter of thought inside, the words, come back with a vengeance.

I am here again, my arm throbbing, the fatigue and mild nausea bearing memories of this morning's treatment. The vividness of experience disappears behind a dark cloud.

I have no answer for the question-about-a-question, and so I mumble: "Whatever you write will do."

Whatever. The students still say I'm cool.

∿

Such lapses seemed to grow in frequency during the fall semester of 1999. Could meditation finally be working? "Just like all the other times," Armine said, "you're suffering premature senility due to dialysis."

But the new fistula was working beautifully. I now ran faster than any deer. Higher blood flows meant better dialysis, and my creatinine dropped to its lowest yet, about twelve (remembering that normal is between .5 and 1.5).

I am back teaching my usual load of four courses. Fatigue and nausea are still companions in the classroom. Health—the feeling of health—has become a faded memory. Hope for the future seems unreal. I enter the clinic each dialysis morning knowing that there is a good probability I might not walk out again. It doesn't seem to matter anymore.

The Cucumber College administration drops hints about release time, reducing my load from four courses to three. Perhaps they have become aware of the creaking specter haunting their hallowed halls. But then, orders came down that any such relief would be subtracted from my salary. I refuse. Enough ego remains to feel hurt.

Armine laughs and says: "You fool! Education is a business like any other. What did you expect?"

I laugh along: "Yup, mental prostitution."

~

And so the year two thousand comes and the world does not go away. Perhaps unconsciously, in one of those timeless moments of peace—"no-mind," Zen would say—I came to terms with my status as a "marginal man." The sensation of having dropped some intolerable burden permeates my being. The headaches subside. I still run each day, but now without regret, laughing and joking, like some holy fool on the dusty Italian roads. Two thousand *is* a new age.

Winter semester begins. Once again, I attempt to teach Eastern Philosophy. But now the words come from a different place, not from the mind, which has fragmented into those lapses, but rather from the gut, perhaps from dead kidneys, perhaps from nowhere.

The students still say I'm "laid back."

~

The phone rings around ten in the evening. I am reading Bernard McGinn's first volume on Western mysticism.

"We have a kidney," says a woman's voice (it was not Sutra Cindi), "but it's a two antigen match."

I hesitate. "Two? Well . . . no."

"Didn't think so." She breaks the connection.

Fifteen minutes later, the phone rings again. This time it's Dr. Jung. "We rechecked," he said. "The match is a three and the organ comes from a *nine-year-old*.

"You ought to take it."

Without thinking, I agree.

A nine-year-old! What if I really thought about it?

Somewhere a nine-year-old has just died. Somewhere, again, lives have been abruptly shattered.

But thinking inhibits action, and too much destroys it.

I'm numb. Dr. Jung gives instructions on when to come (in a few hours), where to go (admissions—again!), what to expect (pre-op). This time I force myself not to think; rather, I immerse myself in the immediate tasks.

I go through the preparations like a sleepwalker. Vaguely I recall this sort of sleepwalking the day I was drafted into the army. Having just graduated college, the draft seemed like a pronouncement of doom. All the work, the education, the hopes were for naught; the Vietnam War would swallow me up as it had so many of my friends.

So now I focus on the moment, neither past nor future, but entirely on the present. Don't ask questions about the child, don't ask about the warrior who just wounded you with a poisoned arrow. Sleepwalk.

On Wednesday, January 26, 2000, at approximately 1 p.m., I was wheeled into pre-op. Everything was familiar—as they say, I knew the drill. The only difference was that right before they took me into surgery, I was given an immune-suppressing drug called cyclosporine. This, of course, would hopefully suppress my body's natural rejection of a foreign organ. The capsules tasted as if they'd been extracted from a live skunk.

Anesthesia was administered. Maxwell's trap door opened and I dropped like lead into that infinite darkness.

∼

I awoke to terrible pain, but not from the incision in my abdomen. My bladder was beginning to fill! Nearly two years on dialysis, and many more in kidney failure, had left an atrophied bladder. But now it had to expand to accommodate urine from . . . *my new kidney!*

A doctor in the recovery room explained the problem and then gave me a small trigger that controls a morphine drip. Soon I was floating away, to Nirvana perhaps.

The pain was "blown out."

Yet, what drug is able to halt the terrible hurricane in my mind? Part of my body is not mine but the organ of a nine-year-old child, recently deceased.

∼

In four days blood toxins dropped to pre-1991 levels. On the fifth day, I came home with a swollen abdomen, a twelve-inch scar, and a new kidney.

And once more, I perceived the flimsiness of language, how words cannot bear the weight of experience. Every light was brighter, each color more brilliant; every taste was pure and honest and every odor sharp. I was like the man in the iron mask, no longer encased in murky, soiled glass, or soaked inside and out with swampy muck. I laughed, I cried, sometimes both at once. Giddiness danced with sorrow; utter joy waltzed with midnight sadness. Like Pythagoras, I heard the Music of the Spheres. A child had to die for such joy.

"You have nothing to feel guilty about," the nurses and doctors told me. The hospital chaplain came to visit. "A child died, but you had absolutely nothing to do with it. Kidney or not, the child died, and would have died."

Yes, perfectly rational.

Yet . . .

Somehow, it seemed obscene to feel happy, even thankful. The hospital staff made perfect sense. But as my bladder filled and the urine flowed (from my kidney, but how could I say my?), reason flowed with it and left me in sadness.

I know . . . my earlier soliloquy about death and death being natural, but how disgusting to say such a thing about a child's death. So much for generalizations! Truly, such a death is the extinction of the future, not simply the end of a temporal life. A child is "not yet," the pure innocence of the yet-to-be in its full contingency. To snuff this out before it begins, before we see what becomes of it, simply seems criminal, god or no god. Innocence of chance doesn't appear innocent. And in this world futures die every day. Many will perish tomorrow.

And yet the joy. In two weeks, ten years dropped from my shoulders. The weightlessness seemed almost unbearable.

Unbearable, undeserved, its price unacceptable, my life has not enough meaning to give meaning to a child's death.

I could not solve the dilemma. Indeed, I could barely live with it. The psychological "child within" is a grotesque caricature of this dilemma.

Nietzsche said, "And when you gaze long into an abyss the abyss also gazes into you."

～

But then, that demon chance—Maxwell—opened his door in the floor. Two weeks out of surgery, with a creatinine of 1.8, I developed a fever, which meant trouble. My immune system had not been suppressed, and acute rejection threatened to destroy the young kidney. However, six days in the hospital, massive dosages of steroids, along with an increase in my normal antirejection drugs, solved the problem. Rejection was rejected.

I came home dazed. Every day I managed to awake without a fever, with a healthy kidney producing urine, was a day I forgot about my dilemma. Something began to happen, like that glorious day in class when thought ceased to flow and serenity seized hold. Perhaps fear of losing my kidney provided the spark. But slowly I made peace with the child within. Somehow, I accepted the unacceptable. It still remained unacceptable, this terrible event that brought a rebirth. Yet, I accepted it with all its ambiguity, its strangeness and chill. It is my personal koan, destroying my reason, to which I have no answer— except, perhaps, to live.

～

Six weeks later, my right leg, the side where the kidney had been transplanted, swelled to twice its normal size. Once again I'd made the elite two percent: In two percent of transplanted patients, a lymphatic pocket develops, causing severe swelling due to entrapped lymphatic fluid.

Lymphocytes are the foot soldiers of the immune system, and my kidney was over-run by them.

A drainage tube was drilled into my abdomen. A bag collecting the fluid was strapped to my leg. The bag filled every few hours and I had to empty it. The swelling went down, but after two days the drainage stopped and the leg swelled again. No amount of readjustment could get the thing working.

The last week of March came and I was back in the hospital. The surgeons huddled with Dr. Jung. One option remained open: to go back into my abdomen and create an "internal drain," which would drain the fluid into the peritoneal cavity. From this site, it would be reabsorbed into the body.

Thus, I was forced to endure another major surgery. They reopened the old incision and built their aqueduct. During the procedure the surgeons examined my new kidney and found evidence of rejection.

Out from surgery, I was taken to the Intensive Care Unit and given one of the most powerful antirejection drugs in the physician's arsenal. The first dose sent me into convulsions. The bombardment of my immune system was scheduled for fourteen days. I grew weaker as each day passed, far worse than any time during kidney failure.

Ten days passed in the hospital. The swelling in my leg slowly subsided, yet creatinine inched upward, reaching 2.5. Then, on the eleventh day, as the shadow of the dialysis machine loomed like a gallows, the creatinine began to fall. By day fourteen, it was 1.9. My child's kidney had been saved.

# Epilogue

More than ten years have passed and with them came new birthdays, or better, *rebirth-days*. I have learned to exist with my unsolved dilemma. I still believe that my new life is not worth the price—like Ivan in Dostoevsky's novel *The Brothers Karamazov*, I wish to give back my ticket. But this, I recognize, is impossible. In the meantime, my numbers have stabilized: Creatinine stands between 1.2 and 0.9, while BUN is around 20. Still on my "ninefold path," I'm treading with lighter feet thanks to the death of a nine-year-old.

The danger, as I perceive it now, is to slowly drift back into the comfortable routines of "normal" life. People say to me: "Aren't you happy to have your life back?" Of course, but habit dilutes astonishment. Every dawn brings surprise, every sunset wonder. I love the changing seasons. Every run is a celebration. The strength slowly returns and no longer do I feel marginal.

The moods still come and go, sometimes with abrupt turns. It could be the steroids. But I find it difficult to remain serious about anything for very long. Meditating each morning I experience the simple yet profound joy of breathing. There is nothing to do, no goal to accomplish. "The bright mirror has no stand," says *The Sixth Patriarch's Dharma Jewel Platform Sutra*. My classroom jokes are worse than ever. I'm very inappropriate.

Teaching has become difficult. My own ignorance is hilarious, and I often think: What if they catch on? There goes a cushy life based upon little effort. Yet, I fear the effects of "education." The students sit there unsmiling, some quite grim, many bored, some narrow-minded and arrogant, most only hoping for a job that pays back the tuition loans and still makes possible a materially comfortable lifestyle. Some have been hurt by life; others are anxious, suspicious, and resentful. Most are jaded. Many teachers are like this too, except they are even more narrow-minded and arrogant. It is nearly impossible to take any of them seriously. Let go, I want to tell them—as Markel said when he died, you already live in the garden.

But they are all too solemn for such words; on the other hand, their truths frighten me. I've decided it is my duty to rebel against that monster "Truth." Maybe I should quit teaching and become a nurse.

Heraclitus said that time is a child idly moving counters in a game. The royal power of Zeus belongs in reality to a child. Whatever significance exists in the universe arises randomly, as that small hand pushes the pieces.

And so there is no conclusion I can offer. All oracles fall silent, all insights fade away. Wisdom itself shatters finally into inarticulate muttering, especially when I stare into that abyss and feel its gaze piercing my heart. Part of me truly is that playful child who desires none of these weighty burdens, that irresponsible nine-year-old playing an incomprehensible game, laughing at wisdom.

And some day, God willing, all of me.

THE END

# About the Author

Dr. Anthony Alioto, professor of history, has served as the Althea W. and John A. Schiffman chair in ethics, religious studies and philosophy at Columbia College since 2002.

Alioto earned a bachelor's degree in history and literature from the University of Wisconsin, and then served in the U.S. Army during the Vietnam War as a personnel specialist. After his military service, he returned to graduate school at Ohio University, where he was a John F. Cady Fellow, earning his master's degree and doctorate in the history of science and philosophy.

Alioto joined Columbia College in 1981. Alioto has been selected as Teacher of the Year, Outstanding Professor of the Year, Faculty Member of the Year and the 1996 recipient of the Governor's Award for Excellence in Teaching. He is the author of *A History of Western Science*. In 2007, Alioto was selected to teach a course entitled "The Buddha and Buddhism" at the Chautauqua Institute in Chautauqua, N.Y. Alioto also teaches for the OSHER Institute for Lifelong Learning at the University of Missouri.

Made in the USA
Lexington, KY
28 October 2012